THE MOVIES QUIZZES

THE QUIZ BOOK COMPANY

First published in 2004 by
The Quiz Book Company Ltd
Bardfield Centre,
Great Bardfield, Essex, CM7 4SL

Copyright © The Quiz Book Company Ltd 2004

2 4 6 8 10 9 7 5 3 1

ISBN 1-84236-504-5

Printed in India

Questions written by Chris Rigby.

QUIZ 1

1 The Black Maria is the name of the world's first-ever movie studio. Who founded it?

2 In what year was The Alamo set?

3 In what capacity did Bombardier Billy Wells appear at the beginning of many pictures?

4 In the world of movie making what is a martini shot?

5 How did Alfred Hitchcock make his usual cameo appearance in the movie Life Boat?

6 What Oscar first was achieved by Julius J. Epstein and Philip G. Epstein in 1943?

7 Who played Jesus in The Greatest Story Ever Told and the Devil in Needful Things?

8 Which actor renamed himself after his hometown of Gary, Indiana?

9 In which film did Ethan Hawke play an incorruptible cop called Jake Hoyt?

10 Which actress played Virginia Wolf in The Hours?

ANSWERS

1. Thomas Alva Edison 2. 1836 3. He banged the Rank gong 4. The last shot of a day's filming 5. In an advert for weight loss 6. First Oscar-winning twins 7. Max von Sydow 8. Gary Cooper 9. Training Day 10. Nicole Kidman

QUIZ 2

. . . .

1 Which 1941 Disney animation told the story of a flying elephant?

2 Which 1980 film comedy saw Gene Wilder sharing a prison cell with Richard Pryor?

3 Who was Harrison Ford portraying on film when piloting the *Millennium Falcon*?

4 Which 1960 film depicted grisly going ons at the Bates Motel?

5 Which film earned Henry Fonda his only Oscar?

6 Who did Clint Eastwood play in the films *The Dead Pool* and *The Enforcer*?

7 Which Bond movie featured a villain called Karl Stromberg?

8 What nationality was Schindler in the film *Schindler's List*?

9 In which film did Clarice Starling rescue Dr Lecter from the clutches of Mason Verger?

10 What name is given to the leading award for the best film at the Venice?

ANSWERS

1. Dumbo 2. *Stir Crazy* 3. Han Solo 4. *Psycho* 5. *On Golden Pond* 6. Dirty Harry Callahan 7. *The Spy Who Loved Me* 8. Austrian 9. *Hannibal* 10. Golden Lion

QUIZ 3

• •

1 What is Brad Pitt's middle name?

2 In 1997, Brad broke off his engagement to which movie star?

3 In which 2000 film did Brad play a gypsy bare-knuckle fighter called Mickey O'Neil?

4 Brad was born in the town of Shawnee, in which US state?

5 In which country did Brad spend seven years, according to the title of a 1997 film?

6 In what year did Brad marry Jennifer Aniston?

7 Who played Brad's police detective partner William Somerset in the film *Seven*?

8 In which 2001 film did Brad play the role of Rusty Ryan?

9 With which actress did Brad share a steamy bedroom scene in *Thelma And Louise*?

10 In which 1994 film did Brad Pitt share a kiss with Tom Cruise?

ANSWERS

1. Bradley, he was born William Bradley Pitt 2. Gwyneth Paltrow 3. *Snatch*
4. Oklahoma 5. *Seven Years In Tibet* 6. 2000 7. Morgan Freeman 8. *Ocean's Eleven* 9. Geena Davis 10. *Interview With The Vampire*

QUIZ 4

• •

Which film features the song…

1 'They Call The Wind Maria'?
2 'Bachelor Boy'?
3 'Raindrops Keep Falling On My Head'?
4 'How To Handle A Woman'?
5 'The Rain In Spain'?
6 'Climb Ev'ry Mountain'?
7 'All That Jazz'?
8 'When You Say Nothing At All'?
9 'Eleanor Rigby'?
10 'Ah Yes, I Remember It Well'?

ANSWERS

1. *Paint Your Wagon* 2. *Summer Holiday* 3. *Butch Cassidy And The Sundance Kid* 4. *Camelot* 5. *My Fair Lady* 6. *The Sound Of Music*
7. *Chicago* 8. *Notting Hill* 9. *Yellow Submarine* 10. *Gigi*

QUIZ 5

• •

Which film co-starred …

1   Michael Caine and Steve Martin as a pair of
    conmen called Lawrence Jamieson and Freddy
    Benson?

2   Tom Hanks and Meg Ryan as Sam Baldwin and
    Annie Reed?

3   Chevy Chase and Dan Aykroyd as a pair of hapless
    spies called Emmett Fitz-Hume and Austin
    Millbarge?

4   James Garner and Tommy Lee Jones as retired
    astronauts Tank Sullivan and William Hawkins?

5   Michael Caine and Ben Kingsley as Sherlock
    Holmes and Dr Watson?

6   Matthew Lillard and Linda Cardellini as Shaggy
    and Velma?

7   Nick Nolte and Eddie Murphy as Jack Cates and
    Reggie Hammond?

8   Graham Chapman and John Cleese as King Arthur
    and Sir Lancelot?

9   Tim Robbins and Morgan Freeman as fellow
    convicts Andy Dufrense and Ellis Redding?

10 Peter Ustinov and Bette Davis as Hercule Poirot
    and Maria Van Schuyler?

ANSWERS

1. *Dirty Rotten Scoundrels* 2. *Sleepless In Seattle* 3. *Spies Like Us* 4. *Space Cowboys* 5. *Without A Clue* 6. *Scooby Doo* 7. *48 Hours or Another 48 Hours* 8. *Monty Python And The Holy Grail* 9. *The Shawshank Redemption* 10. *Death On The Nile*

QUIZ 6

• •

1. In which Oscar winning film did Marlon Brando and Rod Steiger play brothers Terry and Charley Malloy?

2. Who played a teacher called Anna Leonowens in the 1956 musical *The King And I*?

3. Who did David Niven portray in the film *Around The World In Eighty Days*?

4. In which classic western did John Wayne play Ethan Edwards?

5. In which 1954 Hitchcock thriller did James Stewart play a wheelchair bound photographer who witnessed a murder?

6. Who directed the film *Bridge On The River Kwai*?

7. In a 1952 movie, which actor swung around a lamp post whilst singing in the rain?

8. Who played the role of Eve in the film *All About Eve*?

9. Which 1959 film collected eleven *Oscars*?

10. Who played the role of Amy Kane in *High Noon*?

ANSWERS

1. On The Waterfront 2. Deborah Kerr 3. Phileus Fogg 4. The Searchers 5. Rear Window 6. David Lean 7. Gene Kelly 8. Anne Baxter 9. Ben Hur 10. Grace Kelly

QUIZ 7

• •

1   In which 1969 film, adapted from a famous novel, did Peter O'Toole play a teacher called Arthur Chipping?

2   Who played the Cooler King in The Great Escape?

3   In which epic movie did Alec Guinness play Prince Feisal and Anthony Quayle play Colonel Brighton?

4   In which Bond film did 007 first drive an Aston Martin?

5   On whose novel was the 1962 film *To Kill A Mockingbird* based?

6   In which 1964 film did Bing Crosby play Allen-a-Dale?

7   In which 1960 film did John Gavin play Julius Caesar?

8   In which *Carry On* movie did Bernard Bresslaw and Charles Hawtrey play Little Heap and Big Heap?

9   How many *Bond* movies were made in the 1960s?

10 Who did Richard Burton portray in the 1963 film, *Cleopatra*?

ANSWERS

1. *Goodbye Mr Chips* 2. Steve McQueen 3. *Lawrence Of Arabia*
4. *Goldfinger* 5. Harper Lee 6. *Robin And The 7 Hoods* 7. *Spartacus*
8. *Carry On Cowboy* 9. Five 10. Marc Antony

QUIZ 8

1. What was the sub-title of the 2001 *The Lord Of The Rings* movie, the first in the trilogy?

2. How many Oscars did The Return Of The King win in 2004?

3. Which British actor played the role of Theoden in the film trilogy?

4. What is the name Sam short for with regard to the hobbit Sam Gamgee?

5. Who played the evil character of Saruman in the film trilogy?

6. In which country did Peter Jackson direct the *The Lord Of The Rings* movies?

7. Who played the role of Bilbo Baggins in the first film of the trilogy?

8. Which central character was played by Ian McKellan in *The Lord Of The Rings*?

9. Which of the following is the name of a mountain in Return Of The King? Mount Death, Mount Doom, Mount Dread

10. Which actor played the character of Legolas Greenleaf?

ANSWERS

1. The Fellowship Of The Ring 2. Eleven 3. Bernard Hill 4. Samwise
5. Christopher Lee 6. New Zealand 7. Ian Holm 8. Gandalf 9. Mount Doom
10. Orlando Bloom

QUIZ 9

• •

In which film did…

1 Tom Hanks play an FBI agent called Carl Hanratty?

2 Robin Williams play a doctor called Hunter Adams?

3 Ben Stiller play a rabbi called Jake Schram?

4 Robert DeNiro play a fire chief called Lieutenant Donald Rimgale?

5 Sidney Poitier play a teacher called Mark Thackeray?

6 Michelle Pfeiffer play a teacher called Louanne Johnson?

7 Denzel Washington play a lawyer called Joe Miller?

8 Joe Pesci play a lawyer called Vincent Gambini?

9 Mel Gibson play a journalist called Guy S Hamilton?

10 Richard O'Brien play a butler called Riff Raff?

ANSWERS

1. *Catch Me if You Can* 2. *Patch Adams* 3. *Keeping The Faith* 4. *Backdraft*
5. *To Sir With Love* 6. *Dangerous Minds* 7. *Philadelphia* 8. *My Cousin Vinny*
9. *The Year Of Living Dangerously* 10. *The Rocky Horror Picture Show*

QUIZ 10

• •

1 Which 1963 Disney classic features an owl called Archimedes?

2 What type of animal is Kala in Disney's animated version of *Tarzan*?

3 Which cartoon creature has enjoyed film adventures with a honey tree and on a blustery day?

4 What is the home state of Lilo in *Lilo And Stich*?

5 Which film features the characters of Roger, Anita, Pongo and Perdita?

6 What colour is the genie, voiced by Robin Williams in *Aladdin*?

7 What animal is voiced by Bill Thompson in the Disney animation *Alice In Wonderland*?

8 Which 1955 film featured canines called Peg, Jock and Dachsie?

9 In which film did Rowan Atkinson voice the character of Zazu?

10 Which animated heroine saved the life of Captain John Smith?

ANSWERS

1. *The Sword In The Stone* 2. Gorilla 3. Winnie The Pooh 4. Hawaii 5. *101 Dalmatians* 6. Blue 7. The White Rabbit 8. *Lady And The Tramp* 9. *The Lion King* 10. Pocahontas

QUIZ 11

• •

1 Who directed the 1973 film *The Exorcist*?

2 In which 1976 film did Laurence Olivier play a Nazi dentist called Christian Szell?

3 Which 1979 film set during the Vietnam War saw Marlon Brando play the reclusive character of Colonel Kurtz?

4 Which 1974 Mel Brooks comedy was based on a Mary Shelley novel?

5 In which 1979 comedy did Michael Palin play several roles including Pontius Pilate and one of the Three Wise Men?

6 In which 1973 movie did Dustin Hoffman play a forger called Louis Dega, a prisoner of Devil's Island?

7 In which 1976 horror movie did Piper Laurie play the mother of Sissy Spacek?

8 Detective Buddy Russo and Detective Popeye Doyle were partners in which 1971 film?

9 Which 1977 film was advertised with the tag line, "We are not alone"?

10 In which decade was the 1973 film *The Sting* set?

ANSWERS

1. William Friedkin 2. *Marathon Man* 3. *Apocalypse Now* 4. *Young Frankenstein* 5. *The Life Of Brian* 6. *Papillon* 7. *Carrie* 8. *The French Connection* 9. *Close Encounters Of The Third Kind* 10. 1930s

QUIZ 12

1 Who played Susan in the 1985 film *Desperately Seeking Susan*?

2 In which 1984 film did Tom Hanks fall in love with a mermaid?

3 Who played Montgomery Brewster in the 1985 remake of *Brewster's Millions*?

4 What was the title of the 1985 sequel to *Romancing The Stone*?

5 In which 1984 film did Robert Redford play the baseball hero Roy Hobbs?

6 With which song did Tom Cruise serenade Kelly McGillis in the movie blockbuster *Top Gun*?

7 In which 1988 western did Emilio Estevez kill Jack Palance?

8 Which film based on a Willy Russell play saw Joanna Lumley playing a prostitute called Marjorie Majors?

9 Who won a Best Supporting Actress Oscar for her role in the film *Tootsie*?

10 Who won a Best Actress Oscar for her role in the 1984 film *Places In The Heart*?

ANSWERS

1. Madonna 2. *Splash* 3. Richard Pryor 4. *The Jewel Of The Nile* 5. The Natural 6. You've Lost That Loving Feeling 7. *Young Guns* 8. *Shirley Valentine* 9. Jessica Lange 10. Sally Field

QUIZ 13

1 Which 1991 film earned Anthony Hopkins a Best Actor Oscar?

2 In which country was Anthony Hopkins born?

3 Which Prime Minister was portrayed by Anthony in the film *Young Winston*?

4 In which 1993 period drama did Hopkins play a butler called Stevens?

5 Who directed Anthony Hopkins in the 1995 film *Nixon*?

6 Who did Anthony Hopkins portray when Mel Gibson played Fletcher Christian?

7 What was the title of the third film in which Anthony Hopkins played Dr Lecter?

8 Which character was played by Anthony in the 1974 big screen version of *All Creatures Great And Small*?

9 Anthony Hopkins earned an Emmy Award for his portrayal of which leader in the TV production *The Bunker*?

10 In which 1996 film did Anthony play the artist Pablo Picasso?

ANSWERS

1. *Silence Of The Lambs* 2. Wales 3. David Lloyd George 4. *The Remains Of The Day* 5. Oliver Stone 6. Captain William Bligh 7. Red Dragon 8. Siegfried Farnon 9. Adolf Hitler 10. Surviving Picasso

QUIZ 14

· ·

In which city …

1   was the film *Evita* chiefly set?

2   did Dirty Harry do his detecting?

3   was the third *Die Hard* movie set?

4   was the classic movie *The Third Man* set?

5   did Alan Parker direct the movie *The Commitments*?

6   did The Alamo fall to Mexican forces?

7   was the psychological thriller *Don't Look Now* starring Donald Sutherland set?

8   did Robin Williams work as a disc jockey in *Good Morning Vietnam*?

9   were the films *Mary Poppins*, *Oliver* and *The Long Good Friday* all set?

10   was the film *The King And I* set?

ANSWERS

1. Buenos Aires 2. San Francisco 3. New York 4. Vienna 5. Dublin 6. San Antonio 7. Venice 8. Saigon 9. London 10. Bangkok

QUIZ 15

• •

Identify the following films, all of which have titles
  beginning with the letter S

1 In which 1983 film did Al Pacino play a gangster
   called Tony Montana?

2 Which 1989 film starring Pauline Collins was set
   partly on the Greek island of Mykonos?

3 In which 1998 war movie did Ted Danson play the
   cameo role of Captain Frank Hamill?

4 Which 1992 thriller saw Bridget Fonda and
   Jennifer Jason Leigh as flatmates?

5 Linda Lee was the secret identity of which
   eponymous heroine of a 1984 film?

6 Which 1950 film starred Gloria Swanson as a
   movie star called Norma Desmond?

7 Which 2001 romantic comedy co-starred
   Gwyneth Paltrow as Rosemary Shanahan and Jack
   Black as Hal Larson?

8 Which 1999 film featured felines called Snowbell,
   Smokey, Lucky and Red?

9 Which 1993 film starring Richard Gere was a
   remake of The Return Of Martin Guerre?

10 In which 1984 film did Jeff Bridges played an alien
   who lands in the state of Wisconsin?

ANSWERS

1. Scarface 2. Shirley Valentine 3. Saving Private Ryan 4. Single White Female
5. Supergirl 6. Sunset Boulevard 7. Shallow Hal 8. Stuart Little
9. Sommersby 10. Starman

QUIZ 16

• •

1 Henry Hill, Tommy Devito and Jimmy Conway are the three main characters in which 1990 gangster movie?

2 In which 1994 black comedy did Michael Keaton play an editor called Henry Hackett?

3 During which century was the 1995 film Braveheart set?

4 In which 1990 film did Cher and Winona Ryder play mother and daughter Rachel and Charlotte Flax?

5 Which film earned Kevin Spacey an Oscar for his portrayal of Lester Burnham?

6 Who played Vice President Kathryn Bennett in the 1997 action thriller Air Force One?

7 Who played the title role in the 1997 film Mary Reilly?

8 Which 1993 historical spoof was directed by Mel Brooks and set in Sherwood Forest?

9 In which film did Richard Attenborough proclaim, "When they opened Disneyland in 1956, nothing worked"?

10 In which 1999 thriller did Jeff Bridges suspect Tim Robbins of being a terrorist?

ANSWERS

1. *Goodfellas* 2. The Paper 3. 13th century 4. Mermaids 5. *American Beauty*
6. Glenn Close 7. Julia Roberts 8. *Robin Hood – Men In Tights* 9. *Jurassic Park*
10. Arlington Road

QUIZ 17

. . . .

1   What was the title of the 2002 sequel to Analyze This?

2   Which 2002 romantic comedy co-starred Sandra Bullock and Hugh Grant as Lucy Kelson and George Wade?

3   Which 2001 film, set in Liverpool, saw Samuel L Jackson wearing a kilt?

4   Who played the title role in the Oscar winning film The Pianist?

5   Which Oscar winning star made his directorial debut with the 2002 film Antwone Fisher?

6   In which city is the 2001 film Moulin Rouge set?

7   Who won a Best Actress Oscar for her role in the film Monster's Ball?

8   Which 2002 film saw Tom Hanks and Jude Law attempting to kill each other?

9   Which blonde actress wears an eye patch and wields a sword in the film Kill Bill?

10 Which sport features in the 2004 film The Calcium Kid?

ANSWERS

1. Analyze That 2. Two Weeks Notice 3. The 51st State 4. Adrien Brody
5. Denzel Washington 6. Paris 7. Halle Berry 8. The Road To Perdition
9. Daryl Hannah 10. Boxing

QUIZ 18

• •

1   Which song opens the film musical *Grease*?

2   What is the name of the gang led by John Travolta in *Grease*?

3   What is the name of the character played by John Travolta in the film *Grease*?

4   What is the name of the character played by Olivia Newton John in *Grease*?

5   What is the name of the high school that provides the setting in *Grease*?

6   Which song does Frankie Avalon sing in the film?

7   In which year was *Grease* released at the cinemas?

8   Which song did Olivia Newton John sing when wearing skin tight black trousers and a matching low cut top?

9   In the film *Grease* who played the role of Betty Rizzo?

10 In which decade was the movie *Grease* set?

ANSWERS

1. Summer Nights 2. The T Birds 3. Danny Zuko 4. Sandy Olsson 5. Rydell High 6. Beauty School Drop Out 7. 1978 8. You're The One That I Want 9. Stockard Channing 10. 1950s

QUIZ 19

• •

Which films were advertised by the following tag lines?

1 The love affair that shook the world

2 Life is like a box of chocolates, you never know what you're gonna get

3 Real spies .. only smaller

4 Eight legs, two fangs and an attitude

5 They changed her diapers. She changed their lives

6 A husband. A wife. A millionnaire. A proposal

7 If a woman answers, hang on for dear life

8 What if Peter Pan grew up?

9 There can be only one

10 They stole his mind, now he wants it back

ANSWERS

1. Cleopatra 2. Forrest Gump 3. Spy Kids 4. Arachnophobia 5. Three Men And A Baby 6. Indecent Proposal 7. Dial M For Murder 8. Hook 9. Highlander 10. Total Recall

QUIZ 20

• •

1   Which 1985 comedy starred Jimmy Nail and Griff Rhys Jones as a pair of hapless aliens?

2   Who played the Bandit in the 1977 film Smokey And The Bandit?

3   In which 1980 film did Goldie Hawn play a reluctant army recruit?

4   Who played the title role in a 1991 film comedy King Ralph?

5   Who played the role of Josephine in the classic comedy Some Like It Hot?

6   In which 1987 film did Steve Martin profess his love for Daryl Hannah?

7   Which film was advertised with the tag line, "A comedy about sex, murder and seafood"?

8   In which 1998 romantic comedy did Adam Sandler fall in love with Drew Barrymore?

9   Which comedy film sequel was subtitled, When Harry Met Lloyd?

10   Who played the role of Daniel Cleaver in the film Bridget Jones's Diary?

ANSWERS

1. Morons From Outer Space 2. Burt Reynolds 3. Private Benjamin 4. John Goodman 5. Tony Curtis 6. Roxanne 7. A Fish Called Wanda 8. The Wedding Singer 9. Dumb And Dumber 10. Hugh Grant

QUIZ 21

• •

1 What was the first film that featured the song, 'I Will Always Love You'?

2 Which British actor plays Uncle Vernon Dursley in the *Harry Potter* movies?

3 On a film set, who carries the long pole, that holds the microphone in position over the actors?

4 Who married Frank Sinatra in 1966?

5 Which movie director was once quoted as saying, "Actors should be treated like cattle"?

6 Who connects the films *Charlie's Angels*, *Vanilla Sky* and *Gangs Of New York*?

7 Which Disney animation featured the songs, 'A Guy Like You' and 'Sanctuary'?

8 Which was the first Shakespeare play to win a film Oscar?

9 Which film featured a ladies football team called the Hounslow Harriers?

10 Which film star was nominated for an Oscar for a record thirteenth time in 2003?

ANSWERS

1. *The Best Little Whorehouse In Texas* 2. Richard Griffiths 3. The boom operator 4. Mia Farrow 5. Alfred Hitchcock 6. Cameron Diaz starred in all three 7. *The Hunchback Of Notre Dame* 8. Hamlet 9. *Bend It Like Beckham* 10. Meryl Streep

QUIZ 22

1 Which character has been played on film by Olivia de Havilland, Audrey Hepburn and Mary Elizabeth Mastantronio?

2 What does the T stand for in *ET*?

3 Which Nazi was portrayed by Laurence Olivier in the 1985 film *Wild Geese II*?

4 Which film starring Julia Roberts was advertised with the tag line, "She walked off the street into his life and stole his heart"?

5 In which film did Cher play the role of Alexandra Medford?

6 Which 1995 film sequel was sub-titled *The Adventure Home*?

7 Which actor played a hero in the film *Highlander* and a villain in the film *The Avengers*?

8 Whose first film as a twelve year old was entitled Tiger Bay?

9 Which movie star was born Julie Anne Smith?

10 Which Clint Eastwood western took its title from the Biblical book of Revelation?

ANSWERS

1. Maid Marian 2. Terrestrial 3. Rudolph Hess 4. *Pretty Woman* 5. *The Witches Of Eastwick* 6. *Free Willy* 7. Sean Connery 8. Hayley Mills 9. Julianne Moore 10. Pale Rider

QUIZ 23

. . . .

1   In which 2002 thriller did Al Pacino play a sleep deprived detective called Will Dormer?

2   Who did Al Pacino play in The Godfather trilogy?

3   Was Al Pacino born in New York, Chicago or Los Angeles?

4   In which 1990 film did Pacino co-star alongside Warren Beatty and Madonna?

5   What is Al short for in the name of Al Pacino?

6   Which 1992 film saw Pacino working at an eating establishment called The Apollo Café?

7   Which film earned Pacino an Oscar for his portrayal of Lieutenant Colonel Frank Slade?

8   In which 2003 movie did Al Pacino play a CIA operative called Walter Burke?

9   Which 1997 film saw Pacino playing a personification of Satan?

10 In which decade was Al Pacino born?

ANSWERS

1. Insomnia 2. Michael Corleone 3. New York 4. Dick Tracy 5. Alfredo
6. Frankie And Johnny 7. Scent Of A Woman 8. *The Recruit* 9. The Devil's
Advocate 10. 1940s, born in 1940

QUIZ 24

. . . .

In which country were the following film stars born?

1 Marlene Dietrich

2 Kenneth Branagh

3 Greta Garbo

4 Arnold Schwarzenegger

5 Dan Aykroyd

6 Errol Flynn

7 Audrey Hepburn

8 Johnny Weissmuller

9 Gerard Depardieu

10 Keanu Reeves

ANSWERS

1. Germany 2. Northern Ireland 3. Sweden 4, Austria 5. Canada 6. Australia
7. Belgium 8. Romania 9. France 10. Lebanon

QUIZ 25

1 In which film did Doris Day sing *Secret Love*?

2 How many Von Trapp children were there in *The Sound Of Music*?

3 Who wrote the music for the Oscar winning musical *Oliver*?

4 Which song from *High Society* shares its title with a popular TV game show?

5 Which flop musical, set in London, starred David Bowie as Vendice Partners?

6 Who played the role of Maria in the 1961 musical *West Side Story*?

7 Sally Bowles and Brian Roberts were the lead characters in which 1972 film?

8 Which musical features the song *Bless Your Beautiful Hide*?

9 In which musical did Rex Harrison sing, 'I've Grown Accustomed To Her Face'?

10 Which 1958 musical was set in the 1940s in the Solomon Islands?

ANSWERS

1. *Calamity Jane* 2. Seven 3. Lionel Bart 4. *Who Wants To Be A Millionnaire* 5. *Absolute Beginners* 6. Natalie Wood 7. *Cabaret* 8. *Seven Brides For Seven Brothers* 9. *My Fair Lady* 10. *South Pacific*

QUIZ 26

• •

1 Who was the intended assasination target in the war movie *The Eagle Has Landed*?

2 Which equine screen partner of Roy Rogers died in 1965?

3 The films *Pretty Woman*, *Training Day* and *Tango And Cash* were all set in which city?

4 In which 1985 film did Christopher Lloyd appear alongside a dog called Einstein?

5 In which film did Susan Sarandon and Geena Davis drive a car into the Grand Canyon?

6 Who played the title role in the 1968 film *Funny Girl*?

7 In which city was the Disney film *The Aristocats* set?

8 What was the sub-title of the film *Star Trek III*?

9 Who played the estranged wife of Jon Voight in *The Champ*?

10 Which actor connects the films *Blade*, *White Men Can't Jump* and *New Jack City*?

ANSWERS

QUIZ 27

1 In which film, based on a Michael Crichton novel did Yul Brynner play a robotic gunslinger?

2 In which city is the film *Saturday Night Fever* set?

3 Who directed the 1978 horror *Halloween*?

4 Which composer's life story was chronicled in the film A Song To Remember?

5 Who played the title role in the 1996 film *The English Patient*?

6 Who played the role of James Bond in *The Living Daylights*?

7 In which war torn country was the film *Black Hawk Down* set?

8 In which film did Kevin Costner investigate the assasination of the 35th President of the USA?

9 Who plays Professor Severus Snape in the *Harry Potter* movies?

10 In which 1980 film did Dolly Parton, Jane Fonda and Lily Tomlin play co-workers in an office building?

ANSWERS

1. Westworld 2. New York 3. John Carpenter 4. Chopin 5. Ralph Fiennes
6. Timothy Dalton 7. Somalia 8. JFK 9. Alan Rickman 10. Nine To Five

QUIZ 28

• •

1 In what year was the first *Men In Black* movie released?

2 Who played Chief Zed in Men In Black?

3 What is the name of the talking pug dog in the films?

4 Which pop star had a cameo role as Agent M in Men In Black II?

5 What is the name of the cat, central to the plot in the first *Men In Black* movie?

6 Which letter of the alphabet provides the name of the agent played by Will Smith in the movies?

7 Who directed the *Men In Black* movies?

8 What is the first name of Tommy Lee Jones in the films?

9 In which city are the *Men In Black* movies set?

10 Who played an evil alien called Serleena in Men In Black II?

ANSWERS

1. 1997 2. Rip Torn 3. Frank 4. Michael Jackson 5. Orion 6. J 7. Barry Sonnenfield 8. Kevin 9. New York 10. Lara Flynn Boyle

QUIZ 29

• •

Which film star married…

1   Natalie Wood in 1957 and 1972?

2   Dennis Quaid in 1991?

3   Vivien Leigh in 1940?

4   Barbra Streisand in 1963?

5   Sinead Cusack in 1978?

6   Geena Davis in 1987?

7   Kelly Preston in 1991?

8   Prince Rainier of Monaco in 1956?

9   Eddie Fisher in 1959?

10 Daniel Moder in 2002?

ANSWERS

1. Robert Wagner 2. Meg Ryan 3. Laurence Olivier 4. Elliott Gould 5. Jeremy
Irons 6. Jeff Goldblum 7. John Travolta 8. Grace Kelly 9. Elizabeth Taylor
10. Julia Roberts

QUIZ 30

· ·

All ten answers contain the names of Peter, Paul or Mary

1 Who played Evelyn Tremble in the 1967 film *Casino Royale*?

2 Who played the role of Beth Jarrett in the Oscar winning movie *Ordinary People*?

3 Who composed and performed the Bond theme for *Live And Let Die*?

4 Who did Kathy Burke portray in the 1998 film *Elizabeth*?

5 Who played the title role in the 1972 film *The Life And Times Of Judge Roy Bean*?

6 Which actor wore a motorcycle helmet emblazoned with the US Stars and Stripes in the film *Easy Rider*?

7 Which film ended with family members singing 'Let's Go Fly A Kite'?

8 Who directed the films *Green Card*, *The Truman Show* and *Master And Commander*?

9 Who sang Ol Man River in the musical *Showboat*?

10 Who did Douglas Fairbanks Snr marry in 1920?

ANSWERS

1. Peter Sellers 2. Mary Tyler Moore 3. Paul McCartney 4. Queen Mary Tudor 5. Paul Newman 6. Peter Fonda 7. Mary Poppins 8. Peter Weir 9. Paul Robeson 10. Mary Pickford

QUIZ 31

•••••••••••••••••••••••••

1 Which film studios were opened by the Rank Organisation in 1936?

2 Which film features the songs Grow For Me and Dentist?

3 In which country was *The Killing Fields* set?

4 Which city was devastated in the 1974 disaster movie *Earthquake*?

5 What was the first Andrew Lloyd Webber musical to be made into a film?

6 In which film did Clint Eastwood play a street wise cop called Ben Shockley?

7 Who won a Best Actress Oscar for her role in the film *The Three Faces Of Eve*?

8 Which musical instrument did the film character of David Helfgott play in the 1996 film *Shine*?

9 What did Raquel Tejada change her last name to?

10 What was the title of the 2003 sequel to *American Pie* and *American Pie II*?

ANSWERS

1. Pinewood 2. Little Shop Of Horrors 3. Cambodia 4. Los Angeles 5. *Jesus Christ Superstar* 6. *The Gauntlet* 7. Joanne Woodward 8. Piano 9. Welch 10. *American Wedding*

QUIZ 32

. . . .

1 Who played a death row convict called Matthew Poncelet in *Dead Man Walking*?

2 Who links the roles of Gigolo Joe in A.I. and WP Inman in *Cold Mountain*?

3 Which musical set in the 1920s starred Julie Andrews as a flapper girl?

4 Who played the role of Captain Rafe McCawley in the 2001 blockbuster *Pearl Harbor*?

5 What is the title of the 2004 sequel to *The Bourne Identity*?

6 Which city was Nicholas Cage leaving in the title of a 1995 film that earned him a Best Actor Oscar?

7 In which 1996 film did Meg Ryan play a helicopter commander called Captain Karen Emma Walden?

8 In which 2003 family movie did Robert Duvall and Michael Caine play the eccentric uncles of Haley Joel Osment?

9 In which 1975 film did Robert Redford play a stunt pilot?

10 Was the real first name of Bette Davis, Ruth, Rebecca or Rosalind?

ANSWERS

1. Sean Penn 2. Jude Law 3. *Thoroughly Modern Millie* 4. Ben Affleck
5. The Bourne Supremecy 6. Las Vegas 7. Courage Under Fire 8. *Second Hand Lions* 9. The Great Waldo Pepper 10. Ruth

QUIZ 33

• •

1. Who did Jim Carrey portray in the film *Batman Forever*?

2. Who starred as Irene alongside Carrey in the 2000 comedy *Me, Myself And Irene*?

3. What was the alter ego of Stanley Ipkiss in a 1994 film starring Jim Carrey?

4. Which comedy actor directed Carrey in the film *The Cable Guy*?

5. Which 1994 film saw Jim Carrey searching for a dolphin?

6. In which 2003 film did Jim play the role of Bruce Nolan?

7. In which *Dirty Harry* movie did Jim play a rock star called Johnny Squares?

8. In which 1999 film did Carrey play the controversial comedian Andy Kaufman?

9. In which country was Jim Carrey born?

10. What was the last name of Truman in the 1998 Jim Carrey movie *The Truman Show*?

ANSWERS

1. The Riddler 2. Renee Zellweger 3. *The Mask* 4. Ben Stiller 5. Ace Ventura Pet Detective 6. Bruce Almighty 7. *The Dead Pool* 8. *Man On The Moon*
9. Canada 10. Burbank

QUIZ 34

• •

Which TV series starring …

1 Kate Jackson was adapted into a film starring Drew Barrymore?

2 Patrick Macnee was adapted into a film starring Uma Thurman?

3 David Soul was adapted into a film starring Owen Wilson?

4 Peter Graves was adapted into a film starring Tom Cruise?

5 Bill Cosby was adapted into a film starring Eddie Murphy?

6 John Astin was adapted into a film starring Raul Julia?

7 Bill Bixby was adapted into a film starring Jeff Daniels?

8 Roger Moore was adapted into a film starring Val Kilmer?

9 Buddy Ebsen was adapted into a film starring Jim Varney?

10 Robert Stack was adapted into a film starring Kevin Costner?

ANSWERS

1. *Charlie's Angels* 2. *The Avengers* 3. *Starsky And Hutch* 4. *Mission Impossible*
5. *I Spy* 6. *The Addams Family* 7. *My Favourite Martian* 8. *The Saint* 9. *The Beverly Hillbillies* 10. *The Untouchables*

QUIZ 35

• •

The following ten answers are all movies that have titles beginning with the letter M

1 In which 1982 film did David Bowie and Tom Conti play fellow prisoners of war?

2 What was the title of the 1998 film in which Brad Pitt played a personification of death?

3 Which 1990 film earned Kathy Bates a Best Actress Oscar?

4 In which 1989 film did Charlie Sheen play a baseball star called Rick "Wild Thing" Vaughn?

5 Which myopic cartoon character was brought to life on the big screen by Leslie Nielsen in a 1997 movie?

6 Which 1998 Disney film featured the song, 'A Girl Worth Fighting For'?

7 Which 1995 film based on a popular video game saw Christopher Lambert playing Lord Rayden?

8 Which musical features the songs, 'Open A New Window' and 'We Need A Little Christmas'?

9 In which 1974 film did Albert Finney play Hercule Poirot?

10 Which 1978 film saw Brad Davis and Randy Quaid attempting to escape from a Turkish prison?

ANSWERS

1. *Merry Christmas Mr Lawrence* 2. *Meet Joe Black* 3. *Misery* 4. *Major League* 5. *Mr Magoo* 6. *Mulan* 7. *Mortal Kombat* 8. *Mame* 9. *Murder On The Orient Express* 10. *Midnight Express*

QUIZ 36

• •

1 Who played the title role in the 1983 film Silkwood?

2 In which city was Woody Allen born?

3 In which Oscar winning film did Tom Cruise and Dustin Hoffman take a trip to Las Vegas?

4 Which star of the film Spartacus was born Bernard Schwartz?

5 Which actor broke off his engagement to Winona Ryder in 2000?

6 What is the last name of Wayne in *Wayne's World*?

7 In which 1999 spoof sci-fi film did Sigourney Weaver play the role of Lieutenant Tawny Madison?

8 Which actor played the cameo role of Gus Polinski in the 1990 comedy *Home Alone*?

9 Who links the films *Gangs Of New York*, *Star Wars:The Phantom Menace* and *Love Actually*?

10 Which news company was introduced to cinema audiences by a crowing rooster?

ANSWERS

1. Meryl Streep 2. New York 3. Rain Man 4. Tony Curtis 5. Matt Damon
6. Campbell 7. Galaxy Quest 8. John Candy 9. Liam Neeson 10. Pathe
News

QUIZ 37

• •

1 Who was crowned Miss California in 1978 and went on to become a major Hollywood star?

2 In which 1994 comedy did Arnold Schwarzenegger play Dr Alex Hesse?

3 Who played the role of Elena Montero in the 1998 swashbuckler The Mask Of Zorro?

4 For which 1976 film did Faye Dunaway win a Best Actress Oscar?

5 In which 1993 film did Sally Field voice a cat called Sassy?

6 Who directed the 2003 Oscar nominated film Mystic River?

7 In which 1966 film did Paul Newman play Professor Michael Armstrong?

8 Who directed the 2000 film Snatch?

9 In which country was Boris Karloff born?

10 Which actor married the pop star Paula Abdul in 1992 and divorced her two years later?

ANSWERS

1. Michelle Pfeiffer 2. Junior 3. Catherine Zeta Jones 4. Network
5. Homeward Bound 6. Clint Eastwood 7. Torn Curtain 8. Guy Ritchie
9. Great Britain 10. Emilio Estevez

QUIZ 38

• •

1   In the film *The Pink Panther*, what is the Pink Panther?

2   Which British actor played the role of Inspector Quinlan in *The Pink Panther Strikes Again*?

3   Who composed the *Pink Panther* theme music?

4   Who plays the role of Inspector Dreyfus in *The Pink Panther* movies?

5   What nickname was given to the jewel thief Sir Charles Lytton, played by David Niven?

6   Who directed the *Pink Panther* movies?

7   Which of the following is not a Pink Panther movie? *The Curse Of The PP*, *The Mystery Of The PP*, *The Trail Of The PP*?

8   Who played Inspector Clouseau's valet Cato in the movies?

9   What was the title of the first sequel to the *Pink Panther*?

10 What is the first name of Inspector Clouseau?

ANSWERS

1. A large diamond 2. Leonard Rossiter 3. Henry Mancini 4. Herbert Lom
5. The Phantom 6. Blake Edwards 7. *The Mystery Of The Pink Panther*
8. Burt Kwouk 9. *A Shot In The Dark* 10. Jacques

QUIZ 39

• •

In which film did …

1 Robin Williams play Daniel Hillard?

2 Brad Pitt play Detective David Mills?

3 Janet Leigh play Marion Crane?

4 Dan Aykroyd play Mack Sennett?

5 Goldie Hawn play Elise Elliot?

6 Tom Cruise play Lestat de Lioncourt?

7 Eddie Murphy play Billy Ray Valentine?

8 Lee Marvin play Major John Reisman?

9 Gwyneth Paltrow play a young Wendy Darling?

10 Jonathan Pryce play Juan Peron?

ANSWERS

1. *Mrs Doubtfire* 2. *Seven* 3. *Psycho* 4. *Chaplin* 5. *The First Wives Club*
6. *Interview With The Vampire* 7. *Trading Places* 8. *The Dirty Dozen* 9. *Hook*
10. *Evita*

QUIZ 40

. . . .

1 I was born in New York in 1943 and I played the title role in the 1985 film Fletch. Who am I?

2 I was born in Indiana in 1931 and I died in a car crash in September 1955. Who am I?

3 I was born in Los Angeles in 1975 and as a child star I played the role of Gertie in *ET*. Who am I?

4 I was born in New York in 1957 and I married Don Johnson and Antonio Banderas. Who am I?

5 I was born in 1930 and in 1950 I came third in the Mr Universe contest. Who am I?

6 I was born in 1905 and I won a posthumous Oscar for my role in the film On Golden Pond. Who am I?

7 I was born in 1934 and I married my mentor Roger Vadim when I was 18 years of age. Who am I?

8 I was born in Brooklyn in 1939 and I played the FBI boss Jack Crawford in the film Red Dragon? Who am I?

9 I was born in California in 1964 and I am the nephew of Francis Ford Coppola and Talia Shire. Who am I?

10 I was born in Texas in 1949 and I starred in the films The River, In The Bedroom and Missing. Who am I?

ANSWERS

1. Chevy Chase 2.James Dean 3.Drew Barrymore 4. Melanie Griffith
5. Sean Connery 6.Henry Fonda 7. Brigitte Bardot 8. Harvey Keitel
9. Nicholas Cage 10. Sissy Spacek

QUIZ 41

• •

1 Which murderer did Brian Doyle-Murray play in the 1991 film *JFK*?

2 Which star of the TV series *Star Trek:The Next Generation* directed the 2004 film *Thunderbirds*?

3 Who played the role of Smee in the 1991 film *Hook*?

4 Who played the role of Willy Wonka in the 1971 film *Willy Wonka And The Chocolate Factory*?

5 Which series of films features the characters of Wolverine, Sabretooth and Mystique?

6 In which 2000 film comedy did Brendan Fraser sell his soul to the devil?

7 Who played the role of Bobbie Waterbury in the 1970 film *The Railway Children*?

8 In which 1989 film did Sally Field play the mother of Julia Roberts?

9 For which film did Noel Harrison perform the theme song,'The Windmills Of Your Mind'?

10 In which 1999 film did Will Smith play a hired gun called Captain James West?

ANSWERS

1. Jack Ruby 2. Jonathan Frakes 3. Bob Hoskins 4. Gene Wilder 5. *X Men*
6. *Bedazzled* 7. Jenny Agutter 8. *Steel Magnolias* 9. *The Thomas Crown Affair*
10. *Wild Wild West*

QUIZ 42

. . . .

1 In which 1998 animated movie did Val Kilmer voice the character of Moses?

2 Which battle was depicted in the film *They Died With Their Boots On*?

3 Which 1982 musical featured the songs 'It's A Hard Knock Life' and 'Dumb Dog'?

4 Which Bond star was granted the freedom of his home town of Navan in 1999?

5 Which actor made his directorial debut in the 2000 film *Keeping The Faith*?

6 Which member of the Monty Python team directed *The Life Of Brian*?

7 In which *Carry On* film did Kenneth Williams play WC Boggs?

8 In which Yorkshire town was the film Kes set?

9 Which actor was born Christian Hawkins?

10 Which movie icon was once quoted as saying, "When I'm good I'm very good, but when I'm bad I'm better"?

ANSWERS

1. *The Prince Of Egypt* 2. The Battle of The Little Big Horn 3. *Annie* 4. Pierce Brosnan 5. Ed Norton 6. Terry Jones 7. *Carry On At Your Convenience* 8. Barnsley 9. Christian Slater 10. Mae West

QUIZ 43

1 I was born in London in 1933 and called my autobiography What's It All About. Who am I?

2 I was born in Oklahoma in 1962 and I was voted Sexiest Man Alive by People magazine in 2000. Who am I?

3 I was born in Brooklyn in 1920. I married my first wife in 1942 and my eighth in 1978. Who am I?

4 I was born in California in 1944 and in 1975 I founded Industrial Lights And Magic. Who am I?

5 I was born in 1940 and my last film Game Of Death was released after my death in 1973. Who am I?

6 I was born in Surrey in 1908 and died in 1991 seven years after directing my last film A Passage To India. Who am I?

7 I was born in Australia in 1939 and I played James Bond in a 1969 film. Who am I?

8 I was born in Georgia in 1961 and I played Morpheus in the Matrix film trilogy. Who am I?

9 I was born in Los Angeles in 1937 and I played the journalist Carl Bernstein in All The Presidents Men. Who am I?

10 I was born in Kansas in 1895 and I acquired the nickname of the Great Stoneface. Who am I?

ANSWERS

1. Michael Caine 2. Brad Pitt 3. Mickey Rooney 4. George Lucas 5. Bruce Lee 6. David Lean 7. George Lazenby 8. Laurence Fishburne 9. Dustin Hoffman 10. Buster Keaton

QUIZ 44

• •

Unravel the anagrams to give the names of ten Oscar
winning actresses

1 MEANT POSH MOM

2 HIVE VEILING

3 CLARK ELEGY

4 INJURED WALES

5 A POOL SHINER

6 SEA SICK SPYS

7 I SIGHT GEMMA

8 SILENCES A JAG

9 NAKED CLANS JOG

10 FED JOANNA

ANSWERS

1. Emma Thompson 2. Vivien Leigh 3. Grace Kelly 4. Julie Andrews
5. Sophia Loren 6. Sissy Spacek 7. Maggie Smith 8. Jessica Lange 9. Glenda
Jackson 10. Jane Fonda

QUIZ 45

• •

1   In which decade was Marlon Brando born?

2   The film The Island Of Dr Moreau, in which Brando played the title role, was based on the novel of which author?

3   Which film earned Marlon his first Best Actor Oscar?

4   For which film did Marlon refuse to accept a Best Actor Oscar?

5   In which 1955 musical did he play the role of Sky Masterson?

6   In which film did Brando play the leader of a motor cycle gang called The Black Rebels?

7   On whch Beatles album cover did Marlon Brando feature?

8   Who did Marlon Brando portray in the 1953 version of Julius Caesar?

9   In which 1978 film did he play the father of Christopher Reeve?

10 Which character was portrayed by Brando in the film The Mutiny On The Bounty?

ANSWERS

1. 1920s 2. HG Wells 3. *On The Waterfront* 4. *The Godfather* 5. *Guys And Dolls*
6. The Wild One 7. *Sergeant Peppers Lonely Hearts Club Band* 8. Marc Antony
9. *Superman* 10. Fletcher Christian

QUIZ 46

• •

1   Who played the role of Bill the Butcher in the 2002 film, *Gangs Of New York*?

2   The award winning movie *A Man For All Seasons*, telling the story of Sir Thomas More, is set in which century?

3   In which musical did Elizabeth Taylor sing, *Send In The Clowns*?

4   What were Tom, Dick and Harry in *The Great Escape*?

5   Which Jack played Jack Torrance in *The Shining*?

6   Which film co-starring Tom Hanks and Meg Ryan was an updated version of the 1940 film, *The Shop Around The Corner*?

7   In which country was the film director Ang Lee born?

8   Who celebrated his silver wedding anniversary with Joanne Woodward in 1983?

9   Who won a Best Supporting Actor Oscar for his role in the film *Cider House Rules*?

10 The 1985 film, *Sweet Dreams* was a biopic of which country and western star?

ANSWERS

1. Daniel Day Lewis 2. 16th 3. *A Little Night Music* 4. Codenames of escape tunnels 5. Jack Nicholson 6. *You've Got Mail* 7. Taiwan 8. Paul Newman 9. Michael Caine 10. Patsy Cline

QUIZ 47

. . . .

1 In which Bond movie did Kim Basinger play a Bond girl called *Domino*?

2 Which 1969 musical marked the directorial debut of Richard Attenborough?

3 When Miles O'Keefe played *Tarzan*, who played Jane?

4 Who played a conman called Harlee Claiborne in the 1974 disaster movie *The Towering Inferno*?

5 In which film did Tommy Steele sing the song, 'Flash Bang Wallop'?

6 In which 2003 comedy did Steve Martin co-star alongside Queen Latifah?

7 For which film did Carly Simon win a Best Song Oscar with 'Let The River Run'?

8 In which country was the film *Strictly Ballroom* set?

9 Which 1992 film saw Kevin Costner protecting Whitney Houston?

10 In which 2003 romantic comedy did Catherine Zeta Jones play a character called Marilyn Rexroth?

ANSWERS

1. *Never Say Never Again* 2. *Oh What A Lovely War* 3. Bo Derek 4. Fred Astaire
5. *Half A Sixpence* 6. *Bringing Down The House* 7. *Working Girl* 8. Australia
9. *The Bodyguard* 10. *Intolerable Cruelty*

QUIZ 48

1 Who played a teenage Indiana in Indiana Jones And The Last Crusade?

2 What was Indiana searching for in Indiana Jones And The Last Crusade?

3 Who directed the Indiana Jones film trilogy?

4 In which decade was Raiders Of The Lost Ark set?

5 What creatures is Indiana Jones terrified of?

6 In which country was Indiana Jones And The Temple Of Doom set?

7 What is the real first name of Indiana Jones?

8 Who played Indiana's father in Indiana Jones And The Last Crusade?

9 Who played the role of Dr Marcus Brody in the film trilogy?

10 Who played the role of Wilhelmina Scott in Indiana Jones And The Temple Of Doom?

ANSWERS

1. River Phoenix 2. The Holy Grail 3. Steven Spielberg 4. 1930s 5. Snakes
6. India 7. Henry 8. Sean Connery 9 Denholm Elliott 10. Kate Capshaw

QUIZ 49

• •

Unravel the anagrams to give the names of ten Oscar
winning actors

1　HAM KNOTS

2　MINOR JERSEY

3　LION CAGE CASH

4　A MAGIC SHELL DUO

5　A BLURRED VOLT

6　INERT BROODER

7　HANG CAKE MEN

8　WHOA JENNY

9　RODE TIGERS

10　A GROCERY OP

ANSWERS

QUIZ 50

• •

1   I was born in Virginia in 1937 and in 1992 I married Annette Bening. Who am I?

2   I was born in Ireland in 1932 and on film I have played Robinson Crusoe, Don Quixote and Henry II. Who am I?

3   I was born in Kentucky in 1963 and I starred in the films *Donnie Brasco* and *What's Eating Gilbert Grape*. Who am I?

4   I was born in Los Angeles in 1988 and I saw dead people in *The Sixth Sense*. Who am I?

5   I was born in Australia in 1939 and in 1990 I married my film co-star Linda Kozlowski. Who am I?

6   I was born in Los Angeles in 1949 and I played Charles Howard in Seabiscuit. Who am I?

7   I was born in New York in 1932 and I played Norman Bates in four films. Who am I?

8   I was born in Illinois in 1950 and I link *Ghostbusters, Scrooged* and *Groundhog Day*. Who am I?

9   I was born in South Africa in 1975 and my portrayal of mass murderer Aileen Carol won me an Oscar in 2004. Who am I?

10 I was born in Texas in 1945 and I hosted the Academy Awards in 2001 and 2003. Who am I?

ANSWERS

1. Warren Beatty 2. Peter O'Toole 3. Johnny Depp 4. Haley Joel Osment
5. Paul Hogan 6. Jeff Bridges 7. Anthony Perkins 8. Bill Murray 9. Charlize
Theron 10. Steve Martin

QUIZ 51

• •

1   In which 1988 film did Kevin Costner play a baseball player called Crash Davis?

2   Who was born William Claude Dukenfield?

3   In which series of films did Jamie Lee Curtis play the role of Laurie Strode?

4   In which 1993 film did Michael Keaton and Nicole Kidman play man and wife Bob and Gail Jones?

5   Which movie icon was born Maria Magdalena von Losch?

6   In which 1993 futuristic thriller did Sylvester Stallone play the hero and Wesley Snipes play the villain?

7   Alphabetically, who is the last of the seven dwarfs?

8   In which film did Ray Charles sing, Shake Your Tailfeather?

9   Who played the role of Jamal Walker in the 2001 comedy Black Knight?

10 Which 1968 film featured the songs People and I'm The Greatest?

ANSWERS

1. Bull Durham 2. WC Fields 3. Halloween 4. My Life 5. Marlene Dietrich
6. Demolition Man 7 Sneezy 8. The Blues Brothers 9. Martin Lawrence
10. Funny Girl

QUIZ 52

• •

1 Who featured in a nude wrestling scene with Oliver Reed in *Women In Love*?

2 'Up Where We Belong', is the theme song for which 1982 film?

3 Which actor was born William Beedle?

4 In *Carry On* films who links the roles of Dr James Kilmore and Dr Jimmy Nookey?

5 Which 1970s TV show starring Robert Urich became a 2003 film starring Colin Farrell?

6 In which decade was the 2002 film *Chicago* set?

7 Who played the father of Leonardo Di Caprio in Catch Me If You Can?

8 In which Disney animation did Jodie Benson voice the character of Ariel?

9 Which actor played the role of Xander Cage in the 2002 action thriller XXX?

10 Which city saw Eddie Murphy trading places with Dan Aykroyd?

ANSWERS

1. Alan Bates 2. An Officer And A Gentleman 3. William Holden 4. Jim Dale
5. S.W.A.T. 6. 1920s 7. Christopher Walken 8. The Little Mermaid 9. Vin
Diesel 10. New York

QUIZ 53

1 What was the title of the first film in which Tom Hanks co-starred with Meg Ryan?

2 In which country was the film *Saving Private Ryan* set?

3 In which comedy did Tom Hanks and Shelley Long play a married couple called Walter and Anna Fielding?

4 In which film did Tom play the astronaut Jim Lovell?

5 Who played the mother of Tom Hanks in Forrest Gump?

6 In which 1988 film did Tom play the role of Josh Baskin?

7 The 1996 film That Thing You Do, directed by and starring Tom Hanks, told the story of which 1960s pop group?

8 Was Tom Hanks born in Florida, California or Texas?

9 Which film earned Tom Hanks his first Best Actor Oscar?

10 Who played the wife of Tom Hanks in the film The Road To Perdition?

ANSWERS

1. Joe Versus The Volcano 2. France 3. The Money Pit 4. Apollo 13 5. Sally Field 6. Big 7. The Wonders 8. California 9. Philadelphia 10. Jennifer Jason Leigh

QUIZ 54

• •

Identify the film stars that link each group of three
movies

1 *Get Shorty, Batman Returns, Romancing The Stone*

2 *The Hours, The Shipping News, Hannibal*

3 *Alien Nation, The Godfather, Rollerball*

4 *Species, Schindlers List, Sneakers*

5 *Hocus Pocus, Beaches, The Rose*

6 *Bugsy, Reds, Heaven Can Wait*

7 *The Talented Mr Ripley, Elizabeth, The Lord Of The
   Rings:The Two Towers*

8 *The Life Of David Gale, The Usual Suspects, The
   Negotiator*

9 *Zoolander, Meet The Parents, There's Something
   About Mary*

10 *Conspiracy Theory, X Men, Star Trek: Nemesis*

ANSWERS

1. Danny DeVito 2. Julianne Moore 3. James Caan 4, Ben Kingsley 5. Bette
Midler 6. Warren Beatty 7. Cate Blanchett 8. Kevin Spacey 9. Ben Stiller
10. Patrick Stewart

QUIZ 55

1. I was born in London in 1909 and on film I have played Dracula, James Bond and the Scarlet Pimpernel. Who am I?

2. I was born in Ohio in 1968 and I played a character called Sharon Stone in the 1994 film *The Flintstones*. Who am I?

3. I was born in Reading in 1975 and starred in *Iris*, *Quills* and *Heavenly Creatures*? Who am I?

4. I was born in London in 1972 and in the 2004 film The Aviator I played Errol Flynn. Who am I?

5. I was born in California in 1951 and I played the role of Morticia in the 1991 film *The Addams Family*. Who am I?

6. I was born in Brooklyn in 1961 and I had seven different roles in *The Nutty Professor*. Who am I?

7. I was born in Connecticut in 1938 and I played Dr Brown in the *Back To The Future* series. Who am I?

8. I was born in London in 1960 and I link the films *About A Boy*, *Impromptu* and *Sirens*. Who am I?

9. I was born in Washington DC in 1948 and I played Mace Windu in the *Star Wars* movies. Who am I?

10. I was born in New York in 1942. I directed the films *Raging Bull*, *Taxi Driver* and *Casino*. Who am I?

ANSWERS

1. David Niven 2. Halle Berry 3. Kate Winslet 4. Jude Law 5. Anjelica Huston
6. Eddie Murphy 7. Chrostopher Lloyd 8. Hugh Grant 9. Samuel L Jackson
10. Martin Scorsese

QUIZ 56

1 Which A is the title of a film in which Betty Hutton sang Anything You Can Do I Can Do Better?

2 What B is a 1968 film that saw Steve McQueen embarking on a car chase in San Francisco?

3 In which film beginning with C did Woody Allen play Jimmy Bond?

4 In which D film did the character of Johnny Castle join Baby Houseman on the dance floor?

5 Which 1990 film beginning with E featured Johnny Depp with metallic hands?

6 Which 1983 film beginning with F starred Jennifer Beals as a welder and a dancer?

7 In which G movie did Elvis Presley sing 'Return To Sender'?

8 Which 1992 film beginning with H starred Emma Thompson and was based on a novel by EM Forster?

9 In which blockbuster beginning with I did Will Smith and Jeff Goldblum help to foil an alien invasion?

10 In which movie beginning with J did Cuba Gooding Jnr play an American football star called Rod Tidwell?

ANSWERS

1. *Annie Get Your Gun* 2. *Bullitt* 3. *Casino Royale* 4. *Dirty Dancing* 5. *Edward Scissorhands* 6. *Flashdance* 7. *Girls, Girls, Girls* 8. *Howard's End* 9. *Independence Day* 10. *Jerry Maguire*

QUIZ 57

• •

1 Which film beginning with K starred Harrison Ford as a Soviet submarine commander called Alexi Vostrikov?

2 In which movie beginning with L did Roger Moore make his debut as James Bond?

3 Eddie Murphy played a hostage negotiator called Scott Roper in which film beginning with M?

4 In which N movie did Anthony Hopkins play the 37th President of the USA?

5 In which 1987 film beginning with O did Sylvester Stallone play a truck driving arm wrestler?

6 Which 1988 film beginning with P starred Tom Hanks as a standup comedian called Steven Gold?

7 In which Q movie did Peter Ustinov play Emperor Nero?

8 James Dean played Jim Stark in which R movie?

9 Which S movie featured the characters of Doc, Happy, Dopey and four of their co-workers?

10 In which film beginning with T did John Cleese play Robin Hood and Ian Holm play Napoleon Bonaparte?

ANSWERS

1. K 19:The Widowmaker 2. *Live And Let Die* 3. Metro 4. *Nixon* 5. Over The Top 6. Punchline 7. *Quo Vadis* 8. *Rebel Without A Cause* 9. *Snow White And The Seven Dwarfs* 10. *Time Bandits*

QUIZ 58

1 Who voiced the character of Stinky Pete in *Toy Story 2*?

2 What type of animal is Slinky in the *Toy Story* movies?

3 Which toy cowboy was voiced by Tom Hanks in the *Toy Story* movies?

4 What is the name of the young boy who receives Buzz Lightyear as a present?

5 What is the name of the dinosaur voiced by Wallace Shawn in the *Toy Story* movies?

6 What type of bird is Wheezy in *Toy Story 2*?

7 What is the name of the piggy bank in the *Toy Story* movies?

8 Which subsidary of the Disney company makes the *Toy Story* films?

9 Which character is voiced by Don Rickles in *Toy Story*?

10 Who provides the voice for Buzz Lightyear?

ANSWERS

1. Kelsey Grammar 2. Dog 3. Woody 4. Andy 5. Rex 6. A penguin
7. Hamm 8. Pixar 9. Mr Potato Head 10. Tim Allen

QUIZ 59

In which film did …

1. Maurice Chevalier sing 'Thank Heavens For Little Girls'?

2. Christopher Plummer sing 'Edelweiss'?

3. Laurel And Hardy sing 'The Trail Of The Lonesome Pine'?

4. Sid Vicious sing 'My Way'?

5. Howard Keel sing 'Sobbin' Women'?

6. Doris Day sing 'The Deadwood Stage'?

7. Baloo the Bear sing 'Bare Necessities'?

8. Frank Sinatra sing 'My Kind Of Town'?

9. Irene Cara sing 'Out Here On My Own'?

10. Angela Lansbury sing 'The Beautiful Briny'?

ANSWERS

1. *Gigi* 2. *The Sound Of Music* 3. Way Out West 4. The Great Rock And Roll Swindle 5. *Seven Brides For Seven Brothers* 6. Calamity Jane 7. *The Jungle Book* 8. *Robin And The Seven Hoods* 9. *Fame* 10. *Bedknobs And Broomsticks*

QUIZ 60

1 What was the title of the first film that featured the hell raising school of St Trinians?

2 Which British actor played the role of Gerald in *The Full Monty* and the role of *Matt in In The Bedroom*?

3 Which rock group's album provided the soundtrack for the 1982 film *The Wall*?

4 Which British actor born in 1921 acquired the nickname of The British Rock Hudson?

5 In which 1980 film did Bob Hoskins play a brutal London gangster called Harold Shand?

6 Who received Oscar nominations for seven films including The Robe and Beckett, but failed to win any?

7 In which 1996 film did Ewan McGregor play a drug addict called Mark Renton?

8 In which 1993 film did Daniel Day Lewis play Gerry Conlon, one of the members of the Guildford Four?

9 Which comedy actor played the central character of Simon Garden in the 2001 comedy *The Parole Officer*?

10 Which Irish born actor received an honorary Oscar at the 2003 Academy Awards?

ANSWERS

1. The Belles Of St Trinians 2. Tom Wilkinson 3. Pink Floyd 4. Dirk Bogarde
5. The Long Good Friday 6. Richard Burton 7. *Trainspotting* 8. *In The Name Of The Father* 9. Steve Coogan 10. Peter O'Toole

QUIZ 61

1. In which Bond movie did the character of Q first appear on screen?

2. Which star of the film Platoon was born Thomas Michael Moore?

3. Who links the films *The Frighteners*, *Doc Hollywood* and *Casualties Of War*?

4. What type of creatures are the animated characters of Fiver and Dandelion?

5. What was the title of the 2001 sequel to *The Mummy* starring Brendan Fraser?

6. What type of animal features on the logo of MGM Pictures?

7. On whose novel was the 1996 film *Matilda* based?

8. In which 1979 film did Sigourney Weaver appear alongside a cat called Jones?

9. Robert Duvall, Robert DeNiro, Andy Garcia, Al Pacino, Talia Shire and Diane Keaton have all starred in which series of films?

10. In which country was the 1970 film *Ryan's Daughter* set?

ANSWERS

1. *From Russia With Love* 2. Tom Berenger 3. Michael J Fox 4. Rabbits in *Watership Down* 5. *The Mummy Returns* 6. Lion 7. Roald Dahl 8. *Alien* 9. *The Godfather* trilogy 10. Ireland

QUIZ 62

1 Who played Lieutenant John Chard in the 1964 film Zulu?

2 Which 1999 movie set in World War II boasted an impressive cast list including John Travolta, Nick Nolte and Sean Penn?

3 In which film sequel did Edward Furlong play John Connor?

4 On what date of the year is the film *Groundhog Day* set?

5 Who played Jackie Chan's wisecracking partner in the action thriller Rush Hour?

6 Who founded 20th Century Fox?

7 Which 1994 western co-starred Madeline Stowe, Drew Barrymore, Andie McDowell and Mary Stuart Masterson?

8 Which World War II movie chronicled the attack on Arnhem Bridge?

9 What was the Tin Man in search of in *The Wizard Of Oz*?

10 Who played the title role in the 1976 film *Bugsy Malone*?

ANSWERS

1. Stanley Baker 2. *The Thin Red Line* 3. *Terminator II* 4. February 2nd
5. Chris Tucker 6. William Fox 7. *Bad Girls* 8. *A Bridge Too Far* 9. A heart
10. Scott Baio

QUIZ 63

• •

1   In which capital city was Russell Crowe born?

2   Which 2003 film co-starring Russell is subtitled The Far Side Of The World?

3   In which TV soap did Russell Crowe play the character of Kenny Larkin?

4   Who directed Russell in the film *Gladiator*?

5   In which 2000 thriller did Russell co-star with Meg Ryan?

6   Which boxer is portrayed by Crowe in the film *The Cinderella Man*?

7   Is Russell's middle name Ike, Ira or Isaac?

8   Which award winning movie saw Russell playing a mathematician called John Nash?

9   What is the first name of the character played by Crowe in *Gladiator*?

10   In which 1992 low budget movie did Russell play a brutal thug called Hando?

ANSWERS

1. Wellington 2. *Master And Commander* 3. *Neighbours* 4 Ridley Scott
5. *Proof Of Life* 6. Jim Braddock 7. Ira 8. *A Beautiful Mind* 9. Maximus
10. *Romper Stomper*

QUIZ 64

· ·

The answers to the following ten questions have
   initials containing the letters A, B and C

1   BB – Which 1988 film starred Bette Midler and Lily
    Tomlin as twins mixed up at birth?

2   CB – Who links the films The Streetfighter,
    Murphy's Law and Mr Majestyk?

3   CC – Which movie legend married Paulette
    Goddard in 1936?

4   CC – Which movie star appeared in the pop video
    You Can Call Me Al, alongside Paul Simon?

5   AAC – Which comedy duo met The Mummy in a
    1955 film?

6   CB – Who played the title role in the 1998
    historical drama *Elizabeth*?

7   AB – Who married Mel Brooks in 1964?

8   BC – What was the better known name of Robert
    Leroy Parker, played on film by Paul Newman?

9   AAA – In which film did Paul Hogan play the
    character of Terry Dean?

10 CCBB – Which 1968 film featured the song, 'Truly
    Scrumptious'?

ANSWERS

1. Big Business 2. Charles Bronson 3. Charlie Chaplin 4. Chevy Chase
5. Abbott And Costello 6. Cate Blanchett 7. Anne Bancroft 8. Butch Cassidy
9. *Almost An Angel* 10. *Chitty Chitty Bang Bang*

QUIZ 65

• •

In which Carry On movie did …

1 Charles Hawtrey play the character of Private Jimmy Widdle?

2 Phil Silvers play the character of Sergeant Knocker?

3 Sid James play the character of Captain Crowther?

4 Angela Douglas play the character of Annie Oakley?

5 Barbara Windsor play the character of Daphne Honeybutt?

6 Kenneth Williams play the character of Thomas Cromwell?

7 Joan Sims play the character of Calpurnia?

8 Jimmy Thompson play the character of Lord Nelson?

9 Hattie Jacques play the character of Sergeant Laura Moon?

10 Leslie Phillips play the character of King Ferdinand?

ANSWERS

1. *Carry On Up The Khyber* 2. *Carry On Follow That Camel* 3. *Carry On Cruising*
4. *Carry On Cowboy* 5. *Carry On Spying* 6. *Carry On Henry* 7. *Carry On Cleo*
8. *Carry On Jack* 9. *Carry On Constable* 10. *Carry On Columbus*

QUIZ 66

. . . .

1 Who played the villain of the piece in *The Fifth Element*, *Air Force One* and Bram Stoker's *Dracula*?

2 Which Disney film featured a pair of cats called Si and Am?

3 Who played the title role in the Oscar winning movie *Amadeus*?

4 Which swash buckling hero has been played on film by Antonio Banderas, Alain Delon, Tyrone Power and George Hamilton?

5 Which star of the film *Speed* formed her own production company called Fortis Films?

6 Which film adapted from a novel by Umberto Eco starred Sean Connery as William of Baskerville?

7 Which film star was born Jeanette Morrison?

8 Simon Gruber, Colonel Stuart and Hans Gruber are all villains in which series of films?

9 Which Hollywood star formed his own rock band called Dog Star?

10 Which Oscar winning film starring Tom Hanks was based on a novel by Winston Groom?

ANSWERS

1. Gary Oldman 2. Lady And The Tramp 3. Tom Hulce 4. Zorro 5. Sandra Bullock 6. The Name Of The Rose 7. Janet Leigh 8. Die Hard 9. Keanu Reeves 10. Forrest Gump

QUIZ 67

. . . .

1   Who played cops in *Thelma And Louise* and Bad Lieutenant and gangsters in *Mean Streets* and *Sister Act*?

2   Who directed the 1959 film *North By North West*?

3   In which 1998 comedy did Ben Stiller appear alongside a dog called Puffy?

4   Who composed the musical scores for *ET* and *Jaws*?

5   In which 1998 disaster movie did Morgan Freeman play President Tom Beck?

6   Who plays the role of Garth Algar in Wayne's World?

7   Which knighted actor played the Prime Minister of Great Britain in the 2002 comedy Ali G In Da House?

8   Who as a child star played the role of TJ Flynn in the 1979 weepie The Champ?

9   In which African country was the film Out Of Africa set?

10 Which star of the Road movies hosted 18 Oscar ceremonies?

ANSWERS

1. Harvey Keitel 2. Alfred Hitchcock 3. There's Something About Mary
4. John Williams 5. Deep Impact 6. Dana Carvey 7. Sir Michael Gambon
8. Ricky Schroder 9. Kenya 10. Bob Hope

QUIZ 68

• •

1 In which 1985 film did Dolph Lungren play a Russian boxer called Ivan Drago?

2 In which 2001 film did James Toney play the boxer Joe Frazier?

3 Who played the boxer Rubin Carter in the 1999 film The Hurricane?

4 Who played the boxer Billy Flynn in The Champ?

5 Which boxer's life story was chronicled in the film Raging Bull?

6 In which 1956 film did Paul Newman play the boxer Rocky Graziano?

7 In which 1994 film did Bruce Willis play a boxer called Butch Coolidge?

8 What is the title of the 2002 film in which Wesley Snipes plays a boxer called Monroe Hutchens?

9 Who played a boxer called Johnny Walker in the 1988 film Homeboy?

10 What was the title of the 1979 comedy starring Ryan O'Neal as a boxer called Eddie Kid Natural Scanlon?

ANSWERS

1. *Rocky IV* 2. Ali 3. Denzel Washington 4. Jon Voight 5. Jake La Motta
6. Somebody Up There Likes Me 7. *Pulp Fiction* 8. Undisputed 9. Mickey Rourke 10. *The Main Event*

QUIZ 69

Which films were advertised by the following tag lines?

1 He is afraid. He is totally alone. He is three million light years from home.

2 We are not alone.

3 His story will touch you, even if he can't

4 A brutal murder. A brilliant killer. A cop who can't resist the danger.

5 If only they knew she had the power

6 Along time ago in a galaxy far, far away

7 The Man. The Music. The Madness. The Murder. The Motion Picture.

8 Nice planet. We'll take it.

9 Five criminals. One line-up. No coincidence

10 She walked off the street, into his life and stole his heart

ANSWERS

1. *ET* 2. *Close Encounters Of The Third Kind* 3. *Edward Scissorhands* 4. *Basic Instinct* 5. *Carrie* 6. *Star Wars* 7. *Amadeus* 8. *Mars Attacks* 9. *The Usual Suspects* 10. *Pretty Woman*

QUIZ 70

1 What is Private Ryan's first name in the film *Saving Private Ryan*?

2 In which 1996 film did Geena Davis play a secret agent called Charly Baltimore?

3 Who won an Oscar for his portrayal of US Marshal Sam Gerard in the 1993 film The Fugitive?

4 Which 1986 film starred Kirk Douglas and Burt Lancaster as a pair of ageing gangsters called Archie Long and Harry Doyle?

5 Who played Dr Ian Malcolm in *Jurassic Park*?

6 Which 2000 film saw Jon Bon Jovi and Harvey Keitel aboard a German submarine?

7 In which controversial 1994 film did Woody Harrelson play a deranged killer called Mickey Knox?

8 Which San Francisco landmark witnessed the climax of the Bond movie *A View To A Kill*?

9 On whose novel was the film *Jaws* set?

10 Which 2002 war movie starred Nicholas Cage as Sergeant Joe Enders?

ANSWERS

1. James 2. The Long Kiss Goodnight 3. Tommy Lee Jones 4. Tough Guys 5. Jeff Goldblum 6. U - 571 7. Natural Born Killers 8. The Golden Gate Bridge 9. Peter Benchley 10. Windtalkers

QUIZ 71

. . . .

1. What was the uninspired title of the 2002 sequel to 101 Dalmatians?

2. Who is the father of Liza Minnelli?

3. Which famous namee from the world of films penned the book, In Search Of Gandhi?

4. Who played Dr Who in the 1965 film *Dr Who And The Daleks*?

5. Which actor connects the movies *Tequila Sunrise*, *Escape From New York* and *Tombstone*?

6. By what shorter name is Doris Mary Ann von Kappelhoff better known?

7. Which girl band enjoyed a 1984 hit record with the song, 'Robert DeNiro's Waiting'?

8. Which wife of Clark Gable is buried alongside him?

9. In which US city is the 2001 film *Mulholland Drive* set?

10. Who played the role of Aragorn in *The Lord Of The Rings* trilogy?

ANSWERS

1. 102 Dalmatians 2. Vincente Minnelli 3. Richard Attenborough 4. Peter Cushing 5. Kurt Russell 6. Doris Day 7. Bananarama 8. Carole Lombard 9. Los Angeles 10. Viggo Mortensen

QUIZ 72

• •

1   Which birthstone for November provided the title of a 1969 Hitchcock film?

2   In the finale of the film *The Full Monty*, to which song do the heroes shed their clothes?

3   In how many films did Roger Moore play James Bond?

4   Who played the role of Samantha Taylor in the film 10?

5   Which film starring Bette Midler featured the song 'Wind Beneath My Wings'?

6   Which wife of Roman Polanski was killed by the Manson Family?

7   How many Oscars did Steve McQueen win in his acting career?

8   In which animated film did Kenneth Branagh voice a swindler called Miguel?

9   Which of the Marx Brothers was born with the first name Adolph?

10   Which 1974 film sequel won six Oscars?

ANSWERS

1. Topaz 2. 'You Can Keep Your Hat On' 3. Seven 4. Julie Andrews
5. *Beaches* 6. Sharon Tate 7. None 8. *The Road To El Dorado* 9. Harpo Marx
10. *The Godfather Part 2*

QUIZ 73

• •

1 In which series of films did Mel Gibson play the manic character of Martin Riggs?

2 In which animated movie did Gibson voice the character of Rocky the Rooster?

3 What was the title of the 2002 film in which Mel played Reverend Graham Hess?

4 Which 1981 sequel starring Mel Gibson was subtitled The Road Warrior?

5 Which 1992 film saw Mel frozen in suspended animation for fifty years?

6 Which King was played by Patrick McGoohan opposite Gibson's portrayal of William Wallace in Braveheart?

7 Which cocktail provided the title of a 1988 film starring Gibson?

8 In which Australian soap did Gibson play the role of Ray Henderson?

9 Who played the wife of Mel Gibson in the film Ransom?

10 In which US city was Mel Gibson born?

ANSWERS

1. *Lethal Weapon* 2. *Chicken Run* 3. *Signs* 4. *Mad Max 2* 5. *Forever Young*
6. Edward I 7. *Tequila Sunrise* 8. *The Sullivans* 9. Rene Russo 10. New York

QUIZ 74

Are the following statements fact or fib?

1 Christopher Lee who played the Bond villain Scaramanga is the cousin of Bond creator Ian Fleming

2 Gina Lollabrigida was the runner-up in the 1950 Miss Italy contest

3 Lee Marvin is buried alongside the boxer Joe Louis

4 Shirley Maclaine was named after Shirley Temple

5 Nicole Kidman has a morbid fear of cats

6 Roger Moore was 62 years old when he last played James Bond

7 Steve McQueen was a pall bearer at the funeral of Bruce Lee

8 In the film IQ, Walter Matthau played the inventor Thomas Alva Edison

9 Vivien Leigh was born in Kenya

10 Oliver Hardy is a direct descendent of Thomas Hardy, Captain of the HMS *Victory*

ANSWERS

1. Fact 2. Fib, Sophia Loren was runner-up 3. Fact 4. Fact 5. Fib, she does however have a morbid fear of butterflies 6. Fib, he was only 58 7. Fact
8. Fib, he played Albert Einstein 9. Fib, she was born in India 10. Fact

QUIZ 75

. . . .

Which novel by …

1 Alice Walker was adapted into a 1985 film starring Whoopi Goldberg?

2 Irvine Welsh was adapted into a 1996 film starring Robert Carlyle?

3 Boris Pasternak was adapted into a 1965 film starring Omar Sharif?

4 Eric Segal was adapted into a 1970 film starring Ryan O'Neal?

5 Lew Wallace was adapted into a 1959 film starring Charlton Heston?

6 Frank Herbert was adapted into a 1984 film starring Sting?

7 F Scott Fitzgerald was adapted into a 1974 film starring Robert Redford?

8 Mary Norton was adapted into a 1997 film starring John Goodman?

9 HG Wells was adapted into a 2002 film starring Guy Pearce?

10 Truman Capote was adapted into a 1961 film starring Audrey Hepburn?

ANSWERS

1. *The Color Purple* 2. *Trainspotting* 3. *Dr Zhivago* 4. *Love Story* 5. *Ben Hur*
6. *Dune* 7. *The Great Gatsby* 8. *The Borrowers* 9. *The Time Machine*
10. *Breakfast At Tiffany's*

QUIZ 76

• •

1   Who directed the *Godfather* film trilogy?

2   In which 2001 action movie did Owen Wilson play a navy pilot called Lieutenant Chris Burnett?

3   In which country was the 1999 film *The Mummy* set?

4   Which film in the *Star Wars* series was set chiefly on the ice planet of Hoth?

5   For which 1998 blockbuster did Aerosmith record the song, 'I Don't Want To Miss A Thing'?

6   Who played the assasin in the film *The Jackal*, a 1997 remake of *The Day Of The Jackal*?

7   Who won a Best Actor Oscar for his role in the film *My Left Foot*?

8   Which villain did Dr Pamela Isley transform into in the 1997 film *Batman And Robin*?

9   Which 1973 film saw Paul Newman and Robert Shaw playing poker aboard a train?

10 Which villain was voiced by Brian Murray in the Disney animation *Treasure Planet*?

ANSWERS

QUIZ 77

• •

1 In which 1998 action thriller did Will Smith play a lawyer called Robert Clayton Dean?

2 Which 2000 film saw the character of Chuck Noland marooned on a remote island?

3 Which Beatles film featured the songs 'All My Loving' and 'She Loves You'?

4 Which star of the film Kill Bill married and divorced the actor Gary Oldman?

5 Which action movie star was born Chan Kwong Sang?

6 In which city did Glenn Close develop a fatal attraction for Michael Douglas?

7 What type of insects were the villains of the piece in the animated movie *A Bugs Life*?

8 What breed of dog was the movie hero Rin Tin Tin?

9 In which 1998 comedy, set around the sport of American football, did Kathy Bates play the mother of Adam Sandler?

10 Which Oscar winning film starring Woody Allen was sub-titled *A New Romance*?

ANSWERS

1. *Enemy Of The State* 2. *Cast Away* 3. *A Hard Days Night* 4. Uma Thurman
5. Jackie Chan 6. New York 7. Grasshoppers 8. German Shepherd 9. The Waterboy 10. Annie Hall

QUIZ 78

• •

1   In which 1988 film did Hackman play an FBI operative called Agent Anderson?

2   Which 1995 film saw Gene Hackman battling with Denzel Washington for control of a nuclear submarine?

3   In which star studded war movie did Hackman play Major General Sosabowski?

4   In which film did Hackman gain his first Oscar nomination, playing a character called Buck Barrow?

5   In which 2001 comedy did Hackman play the father of Ben Stiller?

6   In which animated movie did Gene Hackman voice the character of General Mandible?

7   In which 1996 comedy did Gene play the father of Calista Flockhart?

8   Which French city provided the connection with New York in *The French Connection* movies?

9   In which 1972 disaster movie did Gene Hackman die aboard a capsized cruise liner?

10 In which 1997 movie thriller did Gene play President Allen Richmond?

ANSWERS

1. *Mississippi Burning* 2. *Crimson Tide* 3. *A Bridge Too Far* 4. *Bonnie And Clyde*
5. *The Royal Tenenbaums* 6. *Antz* 7. *The Bird Cage* 8. Marseilles 9. *The Poseidon Adventure* 10. *Absolute Power*

QUIZ 79

• •

Identify the films in which the following actors wore
   dog collars

1   1994 - Rowan Atkinson

2   1989 - Sean Penn

3   1981 - Dean Martin

4   1976 - Patrick Troughton

5   2000 - Ed Norton

6   1996 - Robert DeNiro

7   1954 - Karl Malden

8   1973 - Max Von Sydow

9   1979 - Rod Steiger

10   1938 - Spencer Tracy

ANSWERS

1. *Four Weddings And A Funeral* 2. *We're No Angels* 3. *The Cannonball Run*
4. *The Omen* 5. *Keeping The Faith* 6. *Sleepers* 7. *On The Waterfront* 8. *The
Exorcist* 9. *The Amityville Horror* 10. *Boy's Town*

QUIZ 80

. . . .

1 What is the family link between the films *The Boston Strangler* and *Klute*?

2 Who did Tony Curtis marry in 1951 and divorce in 1962?

3 In which 2001 film comedy did Catherine Zeta Jones and Julia Roberts play sisters Gwen and Kathleen Harrison?

4 Who is the father of Emilio Estevez?

5 Who co-starred with his wife Kim Basinger in the films *The Marrying Man* and *The Getaway*?

6 Which brothers played brothers in the film *The Fabulous Baker Boys*?

7 Who played the wife of Steve Martin in the film remake of *The Father Of The Bride*?

8 Who played the mother of the baby Mikey in the comedy film *Look Who's Talking*?

9 Which screen siblings co-starred in the film *A Day At The Races*?

10 What is the surname of the brothers that link the films *Independence Day* and *Inner Space*?

ANSWERS

1. The films starred father and daughter Henry and Jane Fonda 2. Janet Leigh 3. America's Sweethearts 4. Martin Sheen 5. Alec Baldwin 6. Beau and Jeff Bridges 7. Diane Keaton 8. Kirstie Alley 9. The Marx Brothers 10. Quaid, Randy and Dennis

QUIZ 81

● ●

1. In which country was the Oscar winning film *The Last Emperor* set?

2. In which 1982 film did the character of Michael Dorsey disguise himself as Dorothy Michaels?

3. In which film did the majority of the action take place in the Kit Kat Club?

4. Who was born Maurice Joseph Micklewhite Junior?

5. The Michael Douglas film *A Perfect Murder* was a remake of which 1954 Hitchcock thriller?

6. Which film sequel to *Babe* featured a Jack Russell terrier called Flealick?

7. In which film sequel did a young Michelle Pfeiffer play a Pink Lady?

8. Which private eye was portrayed by Humphrey Bogart in *The Big Sleep*?

9. In which state of the USA was *Jaws* set?

10. Who wrote the lyrics for the songs in *The Sound Of Music*?

ANSWERS

1. China 2. *Tootsie* 3. *Cabaret* 4. Michael Caine 5. *Dial M For Murder* 6. *Babe 2: Pig In The City* 7. *Grease* 2 8. Philip Marlowe 9. Massachusetts 10. Oscar Hammerstein II

QUIZ 82

• •

1 What was the first film in which Tom Cruise starred with Nicole Kidman?

2 Which Disney animation features the characters of Nani and Cobra Bubbles?

3 Which comedy actor played the lead character of Navin R Johnson in the 1979 film The Jerk?

4 In which 2002 film sequel did Melanie Griffith voice a bird called Margalo?

5 Which star of The Magnificent Seven once said of his own face, "I look like a rock quarry that someone has dynamited"?

6 Which series of sci-fi blockbusters are based on the books of Terry Brooks?

7 Which Disney animated character was named after the Swahili word for lion?

8 Who directed a trilogy of films on the Vietnam War culminating with the movie, *Heaven And Earth*?

9 Which movie mogul was born Lewis Winogradsky?

10 By what shorter name is Major Boothroyd known in the *Bond* movies?

ANSWERS

1. *Days Of Thunder* 2. *Lilo And Stitch* 3. Steve Martin 4. *Stuart Little 2*
5. Charles Bronson 6. *Star Wars* 7. Simba in *The Lion King* 8. Oliver Stone
9. Lew Grade 10. Q

QUIZ 83

• •

1   Is Jodie Foster's real first name Adele, Abigail or Alicia?

2   Who replaced Jodie in the role of Clarice Starling in the film *Hannibal*?

3   In which 2002 thriller did Jodie play the role of Meg Altman, a single mother trapped inside a newly purchased house?

4   In which 1994 western did Jodie provide the love interest for Mel Gibson?

5   Was Jodie born in California, Texas or Florida?

6   In which film did she appear alongside Robert DeNiro playing a character called Iris Steensma?

7   Which film earned Jodie her first Academy Award?

8   In which 1997 film did Jodie Foster play a scientist called Dr Ellie Arroway?

9   In which film did Jodie sing, My Name Is Tallulah?

10 What was the name of the serial killer that Jodie hunted down in *Silence Of The Lambs* with the assistance of Dr Lecter?

ANSWERS

1. Alicia 2. Julianne Moore 3. Panic Room 4. *Maverick* 5. California 6. *Taxi Driver* 7. *The Accused* 8. *Contact* 9. *Bugsy Malone* 10. Buffalo Bill

QUIZ 84

• •

In which film, with a birds name in the title, did …

1 Roger Moore star in 1978?

2 Gregory Peck star in 1962?

3 Pierce Brosnan star in 1999?

4 Bob Hope star in 1939?

5 Michael Caine star in 1976?

6 Jack Nicholson star in 1975?

7 The Marx Brothers star in 1933?

8 Jack Palance star in 1980?

9 Robert Redford star in 1975?

10 James Stewart star in 1965?

ANSWERS

1. *The Wild Geese* 2. *To Kill A Mockingbird* 3. *Grey Owl* 4. *The Cat And The Canary* 5. *The Eagle Has Landed* 6. *One Flew Over The Cuckoos Nest* 7. *Duck Soup* 8. *Hawk The Slayer* 9. *Three Days Of The Condor* 10. *The Flight Of The Phoenix*

QUIZ 85

• •

1 In which film did Harrison Ford play a police detective called John Book?

2 In the 1989 film *Tango And Cash*, who did Kurt Russell play, Tango or Cash?

3 Who played Detective Alex Cross in the films *Kiss The Girls* and *Along Came A Spider*?

4 Who played a cop in the films *The Rookie* and *Sudden Impact*?

5 In which 1990 thriller did Richard Gere play a corrupt policeman called Dennis Peck?

6 Who played the partner of Emilio Estevez in *Stakeout*?

7 Who played a cop in the films *Heat*, *Sea Of Love* and *Serpico*?

8 In which series of comedy movies did Leslie Nielsen play the hapless Lieutenant Frank Drebin?

9 In which decade was the cop thriller *LA Confidential* set?

10 Who played a police detective in the films *Rent A Cop*, *Cop And A Half* and *Sharky's Machine*?

ANSWERS

1. Witness 2. Cash 3. Morgan Freeman 4. Clint Eastwood 5. Internal Affairs
6. Richard Dreyfus 7. Al Pacino 8. Frank Drebin 9. 1950s 10. Burt Reynolds

QUIZ 86

1 In which 1997 blockbuster did Kate Winslet play Rose and Leonardo Di Caprio play Jack?

2 In which 2001 film remake did Tim Roth play the evil character of General Thade?

3 Walter Mathau, John Gielgud and Alec Guinness all died in which year?

4 Who played the role of Max Walker in the 1994 futuristic thriller Timecop?

5 Which 1967 film featured the songs I've Never Seen Anything Like It and The Reluctant Vegetarian?

6 In which 1997 film did Jack Nicholson fall in love with Helen Hunt?

7 Which London born actor played Count Dracula in eleven films?

8 Which city was terrorised by King Kong in the 1933 movie classic?

9 Which Disney animation featured the classical piece of music *The Sorcerer's Apprentice*?

10 Who played the President of the USA in the film *The American President*?

ANSWERS

1. *Titanic* 2. *Planet Of The Apes* 3. 2000 4. Jean Claude Van Damme 5. *Dr Doolittle* 6. *As Good As It Gets* 7. Christopher Lee 8. New York 9. *Fantasia*
10. Michael Douglas

QUIZ 87

• •

1 Which 1995 movie flop starring Kevin Costner lost an estimated $180 million?

2 Which husband of Julie Andrews received a Lifetime Achievement Award at the 2004 Oscars?

3 Who was born Natasha Gurdin and died after falling from a boat in 1981?

4 In which movie did Peter Sellers deliver the classic line, "Gentlemen you can't fight in here. This is the war room"?

5 In which US city is the film *A Streetcar Named Desire* set?

6 Icon Productions, responsible for the 2000 film *What Women Want*, was founded by which Hollywood superstar?

7 Which 1995 film was adapted from a book entitled *Lost Moon* by Jim Lovell?

8 In which 1999 film did Annette Bening play the wife of Kevin Spacey?

9 Which film earned acting Oscars for both Peter Finch and Faye Dunaway?

10 Which pop superstar connects the films *Roustabout*, *Girl Happy* and *The Trouble With Girls*?

ANSWERS

1. Waterworld 2. Blake Edwards 3. Natalie Wood 4. Dr Strangelove 5. New Orleans 6. Mel Gibson 7. Apollo 13 8. American Beauty 9. Network 10. Elvis Presley

QUIZ 88

1 Which villain did Jack Nicholson portray in *Batman*?

2 In which 2003 film did Jack play the role of Dr Buddy Rydell?

3 Who directed Jack in the film *One Flew Over The Cuckoo's Nest*?

4 In which 2003 film did Jack share a bathtub with Kathy Bates?

5 Which cult road movie gained Jack his first Oscar nomination?

6 In which 1992 film did Jack Nicholson face Tom Cruise across a military courtroom?

7 With which movie star did Jack enjoy a 17 year relationship, a liaison that ended in 1990?

8 Which film starring Jack Nicholson was directed by Stanley Kubrick and based on a novel by Stephen King?

9 In which 1976 film did Jack co-star alongside his hero, Marlon Brando?

10 Which 1983 film earned Jack a Best Supporting Actor Oscar?

ANSWERS

1. The Joker 2. *Anger Management* 3. Milos Forman 4. *About Schmidt*
5. *Easy Rider* 6. *A Few Good Men* 7. Anjelica Huston 8. *The Shining* 9. *The Missouri Brakes* 10. *Terms Of Endearment*

QUIZ 89

• •

In which film did Richard Gere play …

1 a cornet player called Dixie Dwyer?

2 a lawyer called Martin Vail?

3 a millionaire called Edward Lewis?

4 a Beverly Hills escort called Julian Kaye?

5 a Chicago cop called Eddie Jillette?

6 a doctor called Sullivan Travis?

7 a lawyer called Billy Flynn?

8 a navy flight school trainee called Zack Mayo?

9 a doctor called Eduardo Parr?

10 a journalist called Ike Graham?

ANSWERS

1. *The Cotton Club* 2. *Primal Fear* 3. *Pretty Woman* 4. *American Gigolo* 5. *No Mercy* 6. *Dr T And The Women* 7. *Chicago* 8. *An Officer And A Gentleman* 9. *The Honorary Consul* 10. *Runaway Bride*

QUIZ 90

1 Which knighted actor narrated the 2000 film The Grinch?

2 How many different roles did Alec Guinness play in Kind Hearts And Coronets?

3 Which disgraced politician was portrayed by Ian McKellan in the film Scandal?

4 Who played the Pope in the 1998 historical drama Elizabeth?

5 Which actor starred in the 2000 films Miss Congeniality and Quills and was knighted in the same year?

6 Which knighted actor played the role of Senator Gracchus in *Gladiator*?

7 Who provided the voice of Prince John in Disney's animated version of Robin Hood?

8 In which 1981 film did Laurence Olivier play Zeus?

9 Which star of the film Ryan's Daughter received a knighthood in 1976?

10 Which actor wore a kilt when he was knighted by Queen Elizabeth II in 2000?

ANSWERS

1. Sir Anthony Hopkins 2. Eight 3. John Profumo 4. Sir John Gielgud 5. Sir Michael Caine 6. Sir Derek Jacobi 7. Sir Peter Ustinov 8. *Clash Of The Titans* 9. Sir John Mills 10. Sir Sean Connery

QUIZ 91

• •

1 Which 2001 thriller saw Cameron Diaz and Penelope Cruz vying for the affections of Tom Cruise?

2 What was the first name of the Blues Brother played by Dan Aykroyd?

3 Which 2001 film starring Ben Affleck was set in 1941?

4 For which Bond movie did Rita Coolidge perform the theme song, All Time High?

5 Who directed the comedy movie Bean starring Rowan Atkinson?

6 Which 1980 movie, directed by Jerry Jameson told the story of a salvage attempt of a ship that sank in 1912?

7 In which 1998 animated movie did Kevin Spacey voice the character of Hopper?

8 In which 2003 romantic comedy did Ewan McGregor and Renee Zellweger play Catcher Block and Barbara Novak?

9 Which movie icon was born Asa Yoelson?

10 Who was the first ever woman to host the Academy Awards?

ANSWERS

1. *Vanilla Sky* 2. Elwood 3. *Pearl Harbor* 4. *Octopussy* 5. Mel Smith 6. *Raise The Titanic* 7. *A Bug's Life* 8. *Down With Love* 9. Al Jolson 10. Whoopi Goldberg

QUIZ 92

1 Who was the only actress to win four Oscars in the 20th century?

2 Who made her debut as M in the Bond movie *Goldeneye*?

3 In which film did Roy Scheider exclaim, "You're gonna need a bigger boat"?

4 Which President of the USA presented Walt Disney with the Presidential Medal of Freedom in 1965?

5 In which 1985 film was the character of Marty McFly bullied by Biff Tannen?

6 What breed of cat is Sassy in the film Homeward Bound?

7 Who directed the 1995 film *Batman Forever*?

8 During which war is the 2003 film *Cold Mountain* set?

9 Which future President of the USA played General George Custer in the film *Santa Fe Trail*?

10 Which actor is the father of the actress Laura Dern?

ANSWERS

1. Katharine Hepburn 2. Judi Dench 3. *Jaws* 4. Lyndon B Johnson 5. *Back To The Future* 6. Siamese 7. Joel Schumacher 8. US Civil War 9. Ronald Reagan 10. Bruce Dern

QUIZ 93

• •

1   In which 1987 film was Arnie a contestant in a
    futuristic game show?

2   Who played the wife of Arnie in the 1994 film True
    Lies?

3   In which 1984 film did Arnie first utter the
    immortal line, "I'll be back"?

4   Which 1988 cop thriller saw Arnie playing a
    Russian state policeman partnered by a Chicago
    cop, played by James Belushi?

5   Which villain did Arnie portray in *Batman And
    Robin*?

6   Which sci-fi thriller was based on the novel
    We Can Remember It For You Wholesale?

7   In which 1985 action fest did Arnie play the role
    of Colonel John Matrix?

8   In what year was Arnie elected Governor of
    California?

9   What was the sub-title of the 1991 movie sequel
    Terminator 2?

10 Which 1987 film saw Arnie battling against an
    alien creature in the jungle?

ANSWERS

1. The Running Man 2. Jamie Lee Curtis 3. Terminator 4. Red Heat 5. Mr
Freeze 6. Total Recall 7. Commando 8. 2003 9. Judgement Day
10. Predator

QUIZ 94

1 In which KK did Fay Wray play the role of Ann Darrow?

2 Which TT played Sir Percy Ware-Armitage in Those Magnificent Men In Their Flying Machines?

3 Which film with the initials FF saw Jamie Lee Curtis playing the mother of Lindsay Lohan?

4 Which PP was portrayed by Michael Palin in The Life Of Brian?

5 Which RR connects the films Brubaker, Legal Eagles and Spy Game?

6 Which MM is the nickname of a movie hero who has the last name of Rockatansky?

7 Which SS was Oscar nominated for her role in the 2001 film In The Bedroom?

8 Which SS played an assassin called Robert Rath in the 1995 film Assassins?

9 Which MM was born Norma Jean Baker?

10 Which GG was born Greta Lovisa Gustafsson?

ANSWERS

1. *King Kong* 2. Terry Thomas 3. Freaky Friday 4. Pontius Pilate 5. Robert Redford 6. *Mad Max* 7. Sissy Spacek 8. Sylvester Stallone 9. Marilyn Monroe 10. Greta Garbo

QUIZ 95

• •

1 Which movie icon was appointed US Ambassador to Ghana in 1974?

2 Who appeared alongside his future wife Lauren Bacall in the film To Have And Have Not?

3 Who won his only Best Actor Oscar for the film Yankee Doodle Dandy?

4 Which movie star was born Virginia Katherine McMath?

5 Who received ten Oscar nominations in her illustrious career for films that included All About Eve and Jezebel?

6 How old was James Dean when he died?

7 In which 1930 film did Marlene Dietrich play a nightclub singer called Lola Lola?

8 Who played Sir Robin of Locksley in the 1938 film The Adventures Of Robin Hood?

9 What was Judy Garland's real first name?

10 Who was born Lucille Fay le Sueur?

ANSWERS

1. Shirley Temple 2. Humphrey Bogart 3. James Cagney 4. Ginger Rogers
5. Bette Davis 6. 24 7. The Blue Angel 8. Errol Flynn 9. Frances 10. Joan
Crawford

QUIZ 96

1 In which decade was Paul Newman born?

2 Who played Danny Ocean in the 1960 film Ocean's Eleven?

3 Who played the role of Muriel in the romantic comedy *Muriel's Wedding*?

4 Which Hollywood superstar produced his own brand of beer called Pale Rider?

5 Pinewood Film Studios is located in which English county?

6 Who played Joey La Motta, the brother of Robert DeNiro, in the film *Raging Bull*?

7 Which actor played a doctor in *Awakenings*, a professor in Flubber and a doctor in *Dead Again*?

8 Which Hollywood superstar was born Thomas Mapother IV?

9 In which seaside resort was the film *Little Voice* set?

10 Who played a lawyer in the film *The Client* and a rock groupie in the film *The Banger Sisters*?

ANSWERS

1. 1920s 2. Frank Sinatra 3. Toni Collette 4. Clint Eastwood
5. Buckinghamshire 6. Joe Pesci 7. Robin Williams 8. Tom Cruise
9. Scarborough 10. Susan Sarandon

QUIZ 97

1. In which 1996 film did Michael Keaton play a cloned character called Doug Kinney?

2. Which 2002 animated horse was known as The Stallion Of The Cimarron?

3. In which film did Michael Douglas play a homicide cop called Nick Curran?

4. How is the character of Norville Rogers otherwise known in the Scooby Doo movies?

5. What has the official name of The Academy Award Of Merit?

6. What breed of dog is the film hero Lassie?

7. Which animator for Monty Python directed the film Twelve Monkeys?

8. Where did Mr Smith go to in the title of a 1939 film?

9. In which 1986 film did William Hurt play a sign language teacher who falls in love with a deaf woman?

10. What was John Wayne's real first name?

ANSWERS

1. Multiplicity 2. Spirit 3. Basic Instinct 4. Shaggy 5. An Oscar 6. Collie
7. Terry Gilliam 8. Washington 9. Children Of A Lesser God 10. Marion

QUIZ 98

• •

1   In which 1998 movie flop did Sean Connery play a villain named August de Wynter?

2   What is Sean Connery's real first name?

3   In which 1995 film did Connery play King Arthur?

4   Which 1987 film earned Sean a Best Supporting Actor Oscar?

5   In which 1996 fantasy movie did Sean voice a dragon called Draco?

6   In which film did Sean Connery make his debut as James Bond?

7   In which Hitchcock thriller did Connery play the character of Mark Rutland?

8   In which city was Sean born?

9   Who did Sean briefly portray in the film Robin Hood, Prince Of Thieves?

10 In which 1989 film did Connery play the father of Dustin Hoffman and the grandfather of Matthew Broderick?

ANSWERS

1. *The Avengers* 2. Thomas 3. *First Knight* 4. *The Untouchables*
5. *Dragonheart* 6. *Dr No* 7. *Marnie* 8. Edinburgh 9. *Richard the Lionheart*
10. *Family Business*

QUIZ 99

In which Bond movie did …

1 Roger Moore dress as a clown at a travelling circus?

2 Sean Connery kill Robert Shaw?

3 Pierce Brosnan kill Sean Bean?

4 Timothy Dalton attend the wedding of Felix Leiter?

5 007 share a bed with Tiffany Case?

6 Adolfo Celi play the villain Largo?

7 007 foil Ernst Blofeld in Japan?

8 007 eject Hugo Drax into outer space?

9 Jaws, a metal mouthed henchman, first appear?

10 Lulu perform the theme song?

ANSWERS

1. Octopussy 2. From Russia With Love 3. Goldeneye 4. Licence To Kill
5. Diamonds Are Forever 6. Thunderball 7. You Only Live Twice
8. Moonraker 9. The Spy Who Loved Me 10. The Man With The Golden Gun

QUIZ 100

. . . .

1 In which 1931 movie did James Cagney play a gangster called Tom Powers?

2 Which 1951 Ealing comedy starred Alec Guinness as a gang leader whose members included Sid James and Stanley Holloway?

3 Who played the title role in the 1963 film *Billy Liar*?

4 In which film did Charlie Chaplin play Adenoid Hynkel?

5 In which film did Dooley Wilson sing 'As Time Goes By'?

6 Who played the title role in *Schindler's List*?

7 Who played the title role in the 1931 gangster movie *Little Caesar*?

8 In which film did Al Jolson sing the songs 'Dirty Hands Dirty Faces' and 'My Mammy'?

9 Who played Bob Hope's leading lady in the *Road* movies?

10 What type of animal was Harvey in the 1950 film *Harvey* starring James Stewart?

ANSWERS

1. *Public Enemy* 2. *The Lavender Hill Mob* 3. Tom Courtenay 4. *The Great Dictator* 5. *Casablanca* 6. Liam Neeson 7. Edward G Robinson 8. *The Jazz Singer* 9. Dorothy Lamour 10. A rabbit

QUIZ 101

• •

1 In the 1949 epic *Samson And Delilah*, who played Samson opposite the Delilah of Hedy Lamarr?

2 Which Hollywood star made his directorial debut with the 2003 film *Confessions Of A Dangerous Mind*?

3 In 2002 Angelina Jolie filed for divorce from which actor?

4 Which 2003 film featured a sailing vessel called the HMS *Surprise*?

5 In which 1954 film did James Mason play the husband of Judy Garland?

6 On whose novel was the film *Far From The Madding Crowd* set?

7 Which 1996 film starred Pete Postlethwaite as the leader of a brass band?

8 Who wrote the screenplays for the films *The Odd Couple*, *California Suite* and *The Sunshine Boys*?

9 In which 1993 film did Denzel Washington play a Washington Herald reporter called Gray Grantham?

10 In which 1999 ghost story did Johnny Depp play Constable Ichabod Crane?

ANSWERS

1. Victor Mature 2. George Clooney 3. Billy Bob Thornton 4. *Master And Commander* 5. *A Star Is Born* 6. Thomas Hardy 7. *Brassed Off* 8. Neil Simon 9. *The Pelican Brief* 10. *Sleepy Hollow*

QUIZ 102

1 In which 1986 comedy did Steve Martin play the wild west character of Lucky Day?

2 Which star of the films *Nikita* and *Stand By Me* died aged just twenty-three in 1994?

3 Who played Robin in the 1995 film *Batman Forever*?

4 Who played the role of General Zod in the film *Superman II*?

5 On whose novel was the 2002 film *About A Boy* based?

6 Who played the President of the USA in the blockbuster movie Independence Day?

7 In which 1978 film did Robert DeNiro play a steel worker called Michael Vronsky?

8 Which 1995 western starred Jeff Bridges as James Butler Hickok?

9 Who played the role of John Bosley in the 2000 film *Charlie's Angels*?

10 In which 1990 film did Shirley MacLaine play the mother of Meryl Streep?

ANSWERS

1. *The Three Amigos* 2. River Phoenix 3. Chris O'Donnell 4. Terence Stamp
5. Nick Hornby 6. Bill Pullman 7. *The Deer Hunter* 8. *Wild Bill* 9. Bill Murray
10. *Postcards From The Edge*

QUIZ 103

• •

1   What was the sub-title of the 1995 action movie Die Hard III?

2   In which TV series did Bruce Willis play the role of David Addison?

3   In which 1990 weepie did Demi Moore play the role of Molly Jensen?

4   What was the title of the 2000 film in which Bruce Willis played a Mafia hitman called Jimmy "The Tulip" Tudeski?

5   Which actor made an indecent proposal to Demi Moore in a 1993 film?

6   In which 1989 film did Bruce Willis provide the voice of Mikey?

7   What is Demi short for in the name of Demi Moore?

8   In which 1999 film did Bruce Willis play a child psychologist called Malcolm Crowe?

9   In which 1997 film did Demi Moore shave off her hair for her role as Lieutenant Jordan O'Neil?

10 In which 2003 animated movie did Bruce voice the character of Spike?

ANSWERS

1. *Die Hard: With A Vengence* 2. *Moonlighting* 3. *Ghost* 4. *The Whole Nine Yards* 5. Robert Redford 6. *Look Who's Talking* 7. Demetria 8. *The Sixth Sense* 9. *GI Jane* 10. *The Rugrats*

QUIZ 104

Which novel by …

1 John Updike was adapted into a 1997 film starring Jack Nicholson as Daryl Van Horne?

2 Louisa May Alcott was adapted into a 1994 film starring Winona Ryder as Jo March?

3 James Dickey was adapted into a 1972 film starring Burt Reynolds as Lewis Medlock?

4 Anita Loos was adapted into a 1953 film starring Marilyn Monroe as Lorelei Lee?

5 Jane Austen was adapted into a 1995 film starring Kate Winslet as Marianne Dashwood?

6 Alistair MacLean was adapted into a 1961 film starring Gregory Peck as Captain Keith Mallory?

7 Margaret Mitchell was adapted into a 1939 film starring Leslie Howard as Ashley Wilkes?

8 Tom Wolfe was adapted into a 1990 film starring Tom Hanks as Sherman McCoy?

9 John Buchan was adapted into a 1978 film starring Robert Powell as Richard Hannay?

10 Stephen King was adapted into a 1976 film starring John Travolta as Billy Nolan?

ANSWERS

1. *The Witches Of Eastwick* 2. *Little Women* 3. *Deliverance* 4. *Gentlemen Prefer Blondes* 5. *Sense And Sensibility* 6. *The Guns Of Navarone* 7. *Gone With The Wind* 8. *The Bonfire Of The Vanities* 9. *The Thirty Nine Steps* 10. *Carrie*

QUIZ 105

. . . .

1　In which country was Omar Sharif born?

2　Who played a vampire called Maximillian in the 1995 comedy horror Vampire In Brooklyn?

3　In which Oscar winning film did Robert Redford play Denys George Finch Hatton?

4　Which spy was played by Michael Caine in Funeral In Berlin?

5　Which musical starring Gene Kelly told the story of a mythical Scottish village that comes to life once every 100 years?

6　In which 1981 film did Kurt Russell play the role of Snake Plissken?

7　Which Steve McQueen movie was introduced with the theme song, 'The WIndmills Of Your Mind'?

8　In which US state was the film *Gone With The Wind* set?

9　Was the actor Richard Harris born in England, Scotland, Ireland or Wales?

10　In which country was the film *Casablanca* set?

ANSWERS

1. Egypt 2. Eddie Murphy 3. *Out Of Africa* 4. Harry Palmer 5.*Brigadoon*
6. *Escape From New York* 7. *The Thomas Crown Affair* 8. Georgia 9. Ireland
10. Morocco

QUIZ 106

• •

1 In which 2000 thriller did Harrison Ford play the husband of Michelle Pfeiffer?

2 What were triffids in the sci-fi thriller *The Day Of The Triffids*?

3 Which star of the sitcom *Taxi* founded his own production company called Jersey Films?

4 The song 'The Best That You Can Do' was an Oscar winning song from which comedy film?

5 What is the connection between the creator of James Bond and the director of *Gone With The Wind*?

6 Which 1997 film grossed over $600 million at the box office?

7 The 1995 film *Clueless* starring Alicia Silverstone, was a modern day adaptation of which Jane Austen novel?

8 In which 1982 film did Dee Wallace Stone play the mother of Henry Thomas?

9 In which 1991 film did Glenn Close have a cameo role playing a pirate called Gutless?

10 In which movie thriller did Jennifer Lopez find herself trapped in the boot of a car with George Clooney?

ANSWERS

1. *What Lies Beneath* 2. Killer Plants 3. Danny DeVito 4. Arthur 5. Fleming, Ian and Victor 6. *Titanic* 7. *Emma* 8. *ET* 9. *Hook* 10. *Out Of Sight*

QUIZ 107

. . . .

1   In what year did Marilyn Monroe die?

2   In which 1986 action thriller did Sylvester Stallone play a street-wise cop called Marian Cobretti?

3   Which film character portrayed by Robin Williams had the first name of Euphegina?

4   Which old west town provided the setting for the film *Gunfight At The OK Corral*?

5   Which 1964 musical starred Audrey Hepburn and was directed by George Cukor?

6   Who played Tarzan opposite the Jane of Maureen O'Sullivan?

7   Which actor died in the films *Reap The Wild Wind*, *The Alamo* and *The Shootist*?

8   Which Oscar winning actor accompanied Bill Clinton to the Labour Party conference in Blackpool in 2002?

9   For which animated film, adapted from a Dickens novel, did Kate Winslet record the song 'What If'?

10 Who played the leading lady of Tom Cruise in the film *Jerry Maguire*?

ANSWERS

1. 1962 2. Cobra 3. *Mrs Doubtfire* 4. Tombstone 5. *My Fair Lady* 6. Johnny Weissmuller 7. John Wayne 8. Kevin Spacey 9. *Christmas Carol: The Movie* 10. Renee Zellweger

QUIZ 108

. . . .

1   In which 1995 film did Michael Douglas play President Andrew Shepherd?

2   In which 1994 film did Michael Douglas accuse his boss, played by Demi Moore, of sexual harassment?

3   Which 2002 film earned Catherine Zeta Jones a Best Supporting Actress Oscar?

4   In which film did Kirk Douglas portray Vincent Van Gogh?

5   Who co-starred with Michael Douglas in two films, playing a writer called Joan Wilder?

6   Which 1958 film co-starred Kirk Douglas and Tony Curtis as half-brothers Einar and Eric?

7   In which country was Catherine Zeta Jones born?

8   Who played a writer and a murder suspect alongside Michael Douglas in the film Basic Instinct?

9   In which 1960 film did Kirk Douglas lead a slave revolt against the Roman Empire?

10 Which 2000 film saw Catherine Zeta Jones co-star with her husband Michael for the first time?

ANSWERS

1. *The American President* 2. *Disclosure* 3. *Chicago* 4. *Lust For Life*
5. Kathleen Turner 6. The Vikings 7. Wales 8. Sharon Stone 9. *Spartacus*
10. *Traffic*

QUIZ 109

. . . .

In which of these animations did …

1 Mike Myers provide the voice of the lead ogre?

2 George Sanders provide the voice of Shere Khan?

3 Phil Harris provide the voice of Thomas O'Malley?

4 Verna Felton provide the voice of the Queen of Hearts?

5 Haley Joel Osment provide the voice of Beary Barrington?

6 Steve Buscemi provide the voice of Randall Boggs?

7 Terry Thomas provide the voice of Sir Hiss?

8 Angela Lansbury provide the voice of Mrs Potts?

9 Emma Thompson provide the voice of Captain Amelia?

10 Karl Swenson provide the voice of Merlin?

ANSWERS

1. *Shrek* 2. *The Jungle Book* 3. *The Aristocats* 4. *Alice In Wonderland* 5. *The Country Bears* 6. *Monsters Inc.* 7. *Robin Hood* 8. *Beauty And The Beast* 9. *Treasure Planet* 10. *The Sword In The Stone*

QUIZ 110

• •

1   Which EC is a 1961 epic in which Charlton Heston played Rodrigo Diaz de Vivar?

2   Which FL directed the 1927 sci-fi movie classic Metropolis?

3   Which film company are represented with a WB logo?

4   Which FO provided the voice of Yoda in the *Star Wars* movies?

5   Which RM narrated the film *Tombstone*?

6   Which JS was directed in four movies by Alfred Hitchcock?

7   Which WH played Pike Bishop, the leader of the Wild Bunch?

8   What O is the last name of Princess Leia?

9   Which HM played the wife of Harrison Ford in the film *Mosquito Coast*?

10 Which MB was nicknamed, The Man of a Thousand Voices?

ANSWERS

1. *El Cid* 2. Fritz Lang 3. Warner Brothers 4. Frank Oz 5. Robert Mitchum
6. James Stewart 7. William Holden 8. Organa 9. Helen Mirren 10. Mel Blanc

QUIZ 111

. . . .

1 Who played the title role in the 1962 biblical epic *Barabbas*?

2 In an alphabetical list, what is the last destination of Bob Hope and Bing Crosby in the Road movies?

3 Who did Dustin Hoffman portray in the film *Lenny*?

4 Which movie mogul and film director is the godfather of Drew Barrymore?

5 Which sport connects the films *Gregory's Girl*, *Fever Pitch* and *Escape To Victory*?

6 Who played the role of Chili Palmer in *Get Shorty*?

7 In which mountain range was the award winning 2003 movie *Touching The Void* filmed?

8 The song 'It Must Have Been Love' by Roxette featured on the sound track of which film starring Julia Roberts?

9 Who played Ferris in the 1986 film *Ferris Bueller's Day Off*?

10 In which 2001 film did Robert Redford play the imprisoned character of Lieutenant General Eugene Irwin?

ANSWERS

QUIZ 112

• •

1 What colour are Superman's boots?

2 What is the nationality of the film director Ingmar Bergman?

3 What was the name of the dog that partnered Detective Scott Turner in a 1989 comedy thriller?

4 Which sleuth solved the crime in *The Mirror Crack'd*?

5 Who played the role of Leo Getz in the *Lethal Weapon* movies?

6 Which action thriller featured bus number 2525?

7 Who played the title role in the 2002 film *John Q*?

8 What type of birds were John, Paul, George and Ringo in *The Jungle Book*?

9 Which arch enemy of the Tracy brothers is played by Ben Kingsley in the 2004 film *Thunderbirds*?

10 Which movie icon married a US marine, a New York Yankee and the author of *The Crucible*?

ANSWERS

1. Red 2. Swedish 3. Hooch 4. Miss Marple 5. Joe Pesci 6. *Speed* 7. Denzel Washington 8. Vulture 9. The Hood 10. Marilyn Monroe

QUIZ 113

1 In which 1979 chiller did James Brolin and Margot Kidder play George and Kath Lutz?

2 Which 2002 film saw David Arquette battling against giant killer spiders?

3 In which 1963 film did the characters of Mitch Brenner and Melanie Daniels meet in a San Francisco pet store?

4 Which 1981 black comedy horror featured a public house called The Slaughtered Lamb?

5 Which 1998 low budget box office smash was set in Maryland Woods?

6 Which director connects the films *Scream* and *A Nightmare On Elm Street*?

7 In which film did Edward Woodward play Sergeant Neil Howie, investigating a crime in the village of Summerisle?

8 Which 1982 film saw the Freeling family's house invaded by ghosts?

9 In which 2004 zombie movie did Simon Pegg play the title character of Shaun?

10 In which 1990 film did Jeff Daniels suffer from a morbid fear of spiders?

ANSWERS

QUIZ 114

• •

Who played the role of …

1   Mr Brown in the 1991 film *Reservoir Dogs*?

2   James Cole in the 1995 film *12 Monkeys*?

3   Robert F Stroud in the 1962 film *The Birdman Of Alcatraz*?

4   Captain Ahab in the 1956 film *Moby Dick*?

5   Melanie Daniels in the 1963 film *The Birds*?

6   Walter in the 2003 film *Second Hand Lions*?

7   Diane Fossey in the 1988 film *Gorillas In The Mist*?

8   Paul Sarone in the 1997 film *Anaconda*?

9   Tom Booker in the 1998 film *The Horse Whisperer*?

10 Sonny Wortzik in *Dog Day Afternoon*?

ANSWERS

1. Quentin Tarantino 2. Bruce Willis 3. Burt Lancaster 4. Gregory Peck
5. Tippi Hedren 6. Haley Joel Osment 7. Sigourney Weaver 8. Jon Voight
9. Robert Redford 10. Al Pacino

QUIZ 115

● ●

1 Which country and western star appeared as himself singing Behind Closed Doors in Every Which Way But Loose?

2 Who played the role of Foxxy Cleopatra in the film Austin Powers In Goldmember?

3 In which film did Lou Diamond Phillips play the pop star Ritchie Valens?

4 Which British pop star connects the films Take Me High, Expresso Bongo and The Young Ones?

5 In the 2002 film John Carpenter's Vampires, who played a vampire hunter called Derek Bliss?

6 Who played the Acid Queen in the film Tommy?

7 Which lead singer of the pop group No Doubt, plays the role of Jean Harlow in the 2004 film The Aviator?

8 Which rocker played Victor Vacendak in the 1992 futuristic thriller Freejack?

9 Which former member of New Kids On The Block played a kidnapper called Cubby Barnes in the 1996 film Ransom?

10 Who played the role of Amber Leighton in the 2002 movie flop Swept Away?

ANSWERS

1. Charlie Rich 2. Beyonce Knowles 3. La Bamba 4. Cliff Richard 5. Jon Bon Jovi 6.Tina Turner 7. Gwen Stefani 8. Mick Jagger 9. Donnie Wahlberg 10. Madonna

QUIZ 116

• •

1   Which 1998 film co-starred Sandra Bullock and Nicole Kidman as the Owens sisters, a pair of witches?

2   Who was originally called Mortimer Mouse?

3   In 1964, which actor represented Egypt in the Olympic Bridge Competition?

4   Who played the wife of Harrison Ford in the film *Patriot Games* and the wife of Michael Douglas in *Fatal Attraction*?

5   Which film featured the Queen hit 'Who Wants To Live Forever'?

6   Who won a Golden Globe for her role of Irene Walker in the film *Prizzi's Honor*?

7   Which Hollywood star provided the voice of Anastacia in the 1997 animated movie?

8   Which *Carry On* movie was released in the USA under the title of Caligula's Funniest Home Videos?

9   Which football star played the role of Monsieur de Foix in the 1998 period drama *Elizabeth*?

10 Which trio were played together on film by Frank Finlay, Oliver Reed and Richard Chamberlain?

ANSWERS

1. *Practical Magic* 2. Mickey Mouse 3. Omar Sharif 4. Anne Archer
5. *Highlander* 6. Kathleen Turner 7. Meg Ryan 8. *Carry On Cleo* 9. Eric Cantona 10. *The Three Musketeers*

QUIZ 117

• •

Who received Oscar nominations for the films …

1 *Glengarry Glen Ross, Dick Tracy* and *The Godfather*?

2 *My Favourite Year, The Stunt Man* and *The Ruling Class*?

3 *The Nun's Story, Wait Until Dark* and *Sabrina*?

4 *The Hours, Far From Heaven* and *Boogie Nights*?

5 *The Quiet American, Sleuth* and *Alfie*?

6 *Othello, Gosford Park* and *A Room With A View*?

7 *The Morning After, On Golden Pond* and *The China Syndrome*?

8 *The Robe, My Cousin Rachel* and *The Spy Who Came In From The Cold*?

9 *Ironweed, A Few Good Men* and *The Last Detail*?

10 *Midnight Cowboy, Tootsie* and *Wag The Dog*?

ANSWERS

1. Al Pacino 2. Peter O'Toole 3. Audrey Hepburn 4. Julianne Moore
5. Michael Caine 6. Maggie Smith 7. Jane Fonda 8. Richard Burton 9. Jack Nicholson 10. Dustin Hoffman

QUIZ 118

• •

The answers to the following ten questions are all film stars that have a surname beginning with the letter A

1 Who was appointed Baron of Richmond Upon Thames in 1993?

2 Which actor made his directorial debut with the 1991 comedy Nothing But Trouble?

3 Who was desperately seeking Susan in a 1985 film?

4 Of whom was it once said, "Can't act, can't sing, slightly bald, can dance a little"?

5 Who won a Best Actor Oscar for his portrayal of Antonio Salieri in the film Amadeus?

6 Who connects the films Paycheck, Forces Of Nature and Changing Lanes?

7 Who links the films Annie Hall, Broadway Danny Rose and The Purple Rose Of Cairo?

8 Which dame played the role of Mrs Moore in the 1984 drama A Passage To India?

9 Who was voted The Worlds Favourite Film Actress at the 1967 Golden Globe Awards?

10 Which movie icon originally performed on the radio as Oklahoma's Yodeling Cowboy?

ANSWERS

1. Richard Attenborough 2. Dan Aykroyd 3. Rosanna Arquette 4. Fred Astaire 5. F Murray Abraham 6. Ben Affleck 7. Woody Allen 8. Peggy Ashcroft 9. Julie Andrews 10. Gene Autry

QUIZ 119

• •

Identify the films from three of the songs from their soundtracks

1 'Boy For Sale', 'It's A Fine Life' and 'As Long As He Needs Me'

2 'Some Enchanted Evening', 'Happy Talk' and 'There Is Nothing Like A Dame'

3 'Mr Snow', 'June Is Busting Out All Over' and 'You'll Never Walk Alone'

4 'We Go Together', 'Freddy My Love' and 'Look At Me I'm Sandra Dee'

5 'I Whistle A Happy Tune', 'Getting To Know You' and 'Shall We Dance'

6 'Gold Fever', 'I Still See Elisa' and 'The Gospel Of No Name City'

7 'Kansas City', 'The Surrey With The Fringe On Top' and 'The Farmer And The Cowman'

8 'The Girl That I Marry', 'You Can't Get A Man With A Gun' and 'Doin' What Comes Naturally'

9 'If You Could See Her', 'Maybe This Time' and 'Mein Herr'

10 'Feed The Birds', 'A Spoonful Of Sugar' and 'Sister Suffragette'

ANSWERS

1. *Oliver* 2. *South Pacific* 3. *Carousel* 4. *Grease* 5. *The King And I* 6. *Paint Your Wagon* 7. *Oklahoma* 8. *Annie Get Your Gun* 9. *Cabaret* 10. *Mary Poppins*

QUIZ 120

• •

1 Who has been played on film by Sarah Bernhardt in 1912, Bette Davis in 1955 and Judi Dench in 1998?

2 Which Disney animation connects the characters of Rafiki and Mufasa?

3 Which film co-starred Steve, Brad, James, Charles, Yul, Horst and Robert?

4 Which actor links the films *Unbreakable*, *Death Becomes Her* and *The Kid*?

5 Which author connects the movies *Congo*, *Timeline* and *Jurassic Park*?

6 What is the connection between the films *Forbidden Planet*, *Kiss Me Kate* and *West Side Story*?

7 Which movie director links the films *Crimson Tide*, *True Romance* and *Top Gun*?

8 Who connects the TV show Ally McBeal with the films *Chicago* and *Charlie's Angels*?

9 Which film role connects Jason Robards, Robert DeNiro and Rod Steiger?

10 Who played the leading lady in the films *Outbreak*, *In The Line Of Fire* and *Get Shorty*?

ANSWERS

1. *Elizabeth I* 2. *The Lion King* 3. *The Magnificent Seven* 4. Bruce Willis
5. Michael Crichton 6. All are based on Shakespeare plays 7. Tony Scott
8. Lucy Liu 9. Al Capone 10. Rene Russo

QUIZ 121

- -

1 What was Blue Thunder in the title of a 1983 action movie?

2 Who wrote the theme song for the Brooke Shields film Endless Love?

3 Who played Jack in the comedy thriller Jumping Jack Flash?

4 What make of car did James Bond drive in Goldeneye?

5 Which movie studio once boasted that they, "had more stars than there are in heaven"?

6 On film who has played The Elephant Man and the jockey Bob Champion?

7 On whose novel is the film Bridget Jones's Diary based?

8 Is Citizen Kane's first name Cedric, Colin or Charles?

9 Who played the role of Hal in the 2001 comedy Shallow Hal?

10 Who is the father of the actor Kiefer Sutherland?

ANSWERS

1. A hi-tech helicopter 2. Lionel Richie 3. Jonathan Pryce 4. BMW 5. MGM
6. John Hurt 7. Helen Fielding 8. Charles 9. Jack Black 10. Donald
Sutherland

QUIZ 122

1 Who played the role of Bullet Tooth Tony in the 2000 film Snatch?

2 Which cult movie and stage show features the transvestite character of Frank N Furter?

3 Which Disney animation features a pair of hapless crooks called Jasper and Horace?

4 The Oscar winning song, You Must Love Me featured in which movie?

5 What colour are the gloves worn by Bugs Bunny?

6 In which series of comedy films does Chevy Chase play the head of the Griswold family?

7 What type of animal is Akela in *The Jungle Book*?

8 Which intrepid movie trio drove a car bearing the registration plate ECTO-1?

9 In which decade did Al Jolson star in the first movie talkie?

10 Christopher Plummer, Roger Moore, Peter Cushing, Michael Caine and Basil Rathbone have all played who on film?

ANSWERS

1. Vinnie Jones 2. *The Rocky Horror Picture Show* 3. 101 Dalmatians
4. Evita 5. White 6. *National Lampoon's* 7. Wolf 8. *The Ghostbusters*
9. 1920s 10. Sherlock Holmes

QUIZ 123

• •

The answers to the following ten questions are all movie stars who have surnames beginning with the letter M

1 Who played the role of Josh Randall in the TV western *Wanted Dead Or Alive*, before finding fame as a movie star?

2 Who did Misty Rowe portray in the film *Goodbye Norma Jean*?

3 Which actor said, "People think I have an interesting walk. Hell I'm just trying to hold my gut in"?

4 When Peter Cook played Sherlock Holmes who played Dr Watson?

5 Who married her long time lover, the film director Taylor Hackford in 1997?

6 Who played the role of Cornelius in the 1967 film *Planet Of The Apes*?

7 Who on film has played the author James Joyce, the banker Nick Leeson and a Jedi knight?

8 Who played the pilot in the 1956 movie *Reach For The Sky*?

9 Which leading lady was born Vera Jane Palmer?

10 Which actor connects the films *Reservoir Dogs*, *Thelma And Louise* and *Mulholland Falls*?

ANSWERS

1. Steve McQueen 2. Marilyn Monroe 3. Robert Mitchum 4. Dudley Moore
5. Helen Mirren 6. Roddy McDowall 7. Ewan McGregor 8. Kenneth More
9. Jayne Mansfield 10. Michael Madsen

QUIZ 124

Are the following statements fact or fib?

1 Demi Moore was once engaged to Emilio Estevez

2 Groucho Marx owned a patent for a wristwatch with a heart monitor

3 Jack Nicholson received Oscar nominations in 1972, 1973, 1974 and 1975

4 Telly Savalas is the godfather of Jennifer Aniston

5 Primrose Magoo was a pseudonym used by Clark Gable

6 Charlie Chaplin was born in London

7 In World War II Christopher Lee worked for the British intelligence

8 In 1998 Clint Eastwood was elected President of the National Rifle Association

9 Marlon Brando, famed for his role in The Godfather, was born on the island of Sicily

10 As a teenager Tom Cruise trained to be a priest

ANSWERS

1. Fact 2. Fib, his brother Zeppo Marx owned the patent 3. Fib, however Al Pacino received nominations in those years 4. Fact 5. Fib, the pseudonym was used by WC Fields 6. Fact 7. Fact 8. Fib, this post went to Charlton Heston 9. Fib, he was born in the US state of Nebraska 10. Fact

QUIZ 125

• •

1. For which 1986 film directed by Woody Allen did Michael Caine win a Best Supporting Actor Oscar?

2. Who won a BAFTA for his role of Charles in *Four Weddings And A Funeral*?

3. Which film won Dustin Hoffman his second Best Actor Oscar?

4. Which actor won an Oscar for Best Original Screenplay for the film *Good Will Hunting*?

5. Which 1992 film earned Clint Eastwood a Best Director Oscar?

6. Who were the first husband and wife to win separate acting Oscars?

7. Who won a Best Actor Oscar for his role in The Goodbye Girl?

8. Michael Landau won a Best Supporting Actor Oscar for his portrayal of which horror movie star in the film Ed Wood?

9. Which British actor won an Oscar for his portrayal of Claus Von Bulow?

10. Who won a Best Actress Oscar for the film Monsters Ball?

ANSWERS

1. Hannah And Her Sisters 2. Hugh Grant 3. Rain Man 4. Matt Damon 5. Unforgiven 6. Laurence Olivier and Vivien Leigh 7. Richard Dreyfuss 8. Bela Lugosi 9. Jeremy Irons 10. Halle Berry

QUIZ 126

1 In which film did Laurence Fishburne say, "You are the one Neo"?

2 In which Canadian city was John Candy born?

3 Which leading box office star founded her own production company called Shoelace Productions?

4 In which city was Universal Pictures founded in 1912?

5 What do the initials PG signify with regard to film classifications?

6 Which singer played the role of Nathan Detroit in the 1959 musical *Guys And Dolls*?

7 In which film did Steve McQueen drive a 390 GT Ford Mustang?

8 Who played the Bond villain Max Zorin in *A View To A Kill*?

9 Who was the first film star to win a Best Actor Oscar in consecutive years?

10 Who split from her husband Dennis Quaid, following a highly publicised affair with Russell Crowe?

ANSWERS

1. *The Matrix* 2. Toronto 3. Julia Roberts 4. Chicago 5. Parental Guidance
6. Frank Sinatra 7. *Bullitt* 8. Christopher Walken 9. Spencer Tracy 10. Meg Ryan

QUIZ 127

• •

1 Which of the Marx Brothers never spoke on film?

2 The film *A Night To Remember* was based on which historical event of the 20th century?

3 Who was Humphrey Bogart's leading lady in the movie classic *Casablanca*?

4 In which decade was the 2001 drama *Gosford Park* set?

5 What is the sub-title of *Star Wars* Episode II?

6 Which star of the TV show The Sopranos played a brutal prison governor called Colonel Winter in *The Last Castle*?

7 Which 1984 film featured a T - 800 robot?

8 Selina Kyle is the secret identity of which character in *Batman Returns*?

9 Who directed the films *Trading Places* and *The Blues Brothers*?

10 Which US star played the villain Pascal Sauvage in the 2003 spy comedy *Johnny English*?

ANSWERS

1. Harpo 2. The sinking of the Titanic 3. Ingrid Bergman 4. 1930s 5. *Attack Of The Clones* 6. James Gandolfini 7. *Terminator* 8. Catwoman 9. John Landis 10. John Malcovich

QUIZ 128

• •

Identify the famous names from the world of films
from their nicknames and their initials

1 RR - The King of the Cowboys

2 BB - The Pout

3 LT - The Sweater Girl

4 JC - Cranberry

5 LC - The Man Of A Thousand Faces

6 JH - The Platinum Blonde

7 AH - The Master of Suspense

8 CC - The Little Tramp

9 RH - The Love Goddess

10 RB - The Voice

ANSWERS

1. Roy Rogers 2. Brigitte Bardot 3. Lana Turner 4. Joan Crawford 5. Lon
Chaney 6. Jean Harlow 7. Alfred Hitchcock 8. Charlie Chaplin 9. Rita
Hayworth 10. Richard Burton

QUIZ 129

• •

In which …

1   2001 film did Ewan McGregor kiss Nicole Kidman?

2   1973 film did Robert Redford kiss Barbra Streisand?

3   1986 film did Tom Cruise kiss Kelly McGillis?

4   1966 film did Michael Caine kiss Shelley Winters?

5   1981 film did Jack Nicholson kiss Jessica Lange?

6   1934 film did Clark Gable kiss Claudette Colbert?

7   1988 film did Harrison Ford kiss Melanie Griffith?

8   1997 film did Mel Gibson kiss Julia Roberts?

9   2003 film did Orlando Bloom kiss Keira Knightley?

10 1973 film did Paul Newman kiss Eileen Brennan?

ANSWERS

1. *Moulin Rouge* 2. *The Way We Were* 3. *Top Gun* 4. *Alfie* 5. *The Postman Always Rings Twice* 6. *It Happened One Night* 7. *Working Girl* 8. *Conspiracy Theory* 9. *The Pirates Of The Caribbean* 10. *The Sting*

QUIZ 130

• •

1   Is Richard Gere's middle name Tarquin, Tiffany or Tiberius?

2   How many women won a Best Director Oscar in the 20th century, none, one or two?

3   Was Rudolph Valentino 21, 31 or 41 when he died?

4   Who plays the author JM Barrie in the 2004 film JM Barrie's Neverland. Is it Johnny Depp, Ed Norton or Ethan Hawke?

5   Was Al Jolson born in Latvia, Lithuania or Liberia?

6   Is Cary Grant's real first name Arthur, Aristotle or Archibald?

7   Was Orson Welles 25, 30 or 35 when he made his film debut with Citizen Kane?

8   Which is the longest film Ben Hur, Dances With Wolves or Gone With The Wind?

9   How many Oscar nominations did the 1997 film *Titanic* receive, 12, 13 or 14?

10 What does the F stand for in the name of the actor F Murray Abraham. Fauntleroy, Frederico or Fahrid?

ANSWERS

1. Tiffany 2. None 3. 31 4. Johnny Depp 5. Lithuania 6. Archibald 7. 25
8. Gone With The Wind at 231 minutes 9. 14 10. Fahrid

QUIZ 131

. . . .

1   In which city was Brigitte Bardot born?

2   Who played Lee Harvey Oswald in the 1991 film JFK?

3   In which decade was the 1967 film Bonnie And Clyde chiefly set?

4   What is the name of the cowgirl in *Toy Story 2*?

5   In which 1992 film did Daniel Day Lewis play the role of Hawkeye?

6   Which author has been played on film by Stephen Fry and Peter Finch?

7   Which star of the films *The Great Escape* and *Space Cowboys* won a Purple Heart in the Korean War?

8   Who won a Golden Globe for his performance in the film *Little Voice*?

9   Which 1987 film starring Oliver Reed was set on a desert island and based on a novel by Lucy Irving?

10 Which violent 1971 movie starring Dustin Hoffman was based on a novel entitled *The Siege Of Trencher's Farm*?

ANSWERS

1. Paris 2. Gary Oldman 3. 1930s 4. Jessie 5.*Last Of The Mohicans* 6.Oscar Wilde 7.James Garner 8. Michael Caine 9. *Castaway* 10. *Straw Dogs*

QUIZ 132

1 Which husband and wife link the films *The Man With Two Brains* and *Superman*?

2 In which country was the actor Anthony Quinn born?

3 In the 1993 swashbuckler *The Three Musketeers*, who played Aramis opposite the Athos of Kiefer Sutherland?

4 In which 2000 film did Julia Roberts play a legal assistant battling against a Californian power company?

5 In which 2001 film did Toby Maguire and Susan Sarandon voice dogs called Lou and Ivy?

6 Name the son of Bruce Lee, who was killed while filming the movie *The Crow*.

7 In which 2003 comedy did Eddie Murphy visit a haunted house with his family?

8 Which comedy duo starred in the films *The Intelligence Men* and *The Magnificent Two*?

9 Which Irish actor's 2002 funeral was attended by Russell Crowe and snooker champion Alex Higgins?

10 Which former husband and wife connect the films *Jurassic Park* and *Thelma And Louise*?

ANSWERS

1. Steve Martin and Victoria Tennant 2. Mexico 3. Charlie Sheen 4. *Erin Brockovich* 5. *Cats And Dogs* 6. Brandon Lee 7. Haunted Mansion 8. Morecambe & Wise 9. Richard Harris 10. Jeff Goldblum and Geena Davis

QUIZ 133

. . . .

The answers to the following ten questions are all films beginning with the letter F

1 Which 2001 film featured Johnny Depp investigating the murders of Jack The Ripper?

2 Which 1997 comedy co-starred John Cleese, Michael Palin and Ronnie Corbett as fellow zoo employees?

3 Which Bond theme was performed by Matt Monro?

4 In which 1981 film did Paul Newman play a uniformed cop called Officer Murphy?

5 Which 1972 Alfred Hitchcock thriller starred Barry Foster as a killer called Robert Rusk?

6 Which musical features the songs Tradition and Matchmaker?

7 Which 1987 Vietnam War movie was directed by Stanley Kubrick and starred Matthew Modine?

8 In which 1993 film did Michael Douglas embark on a gun toting rampage through Los Angeles?

9 Jason Lives and Jason Takes Manhattan were two of the many sequels of which slash horror movie?

10 In which film did Frances McDormand play a pregnant police chief called Marge Gunderson?

ANSWERS

1. *From Hell* 2. *Fierce Creatures* 3. *From Russia With Love* 4. *Fort Apache The Bronx* 5. *Frenzy* 6. *Fiddler On The Roof* 7. *Full Metal Jacket* 8. *Falling Down* 9. *Friday The 13th* 10. *Fargo*

QUIZ 134

. . . .

Identify the film stars from their real names and initials

1 YB - Taidje Khan

2 BS - Ruby Stevens

3 BD - Mary Cathleen Collins

4 RM - Reginald Truscott - Jones

5 GW - Jerome Silberman

6 KS - Kevin Fowler

7 SL - Arthur Jefferson

8 RH - Roy Scherer

9 BB - Camille Javal

10 MP - Gladys Smith

ANSWERS

1. Yul Brynner 2. Barbara Stanwyck 3. Bo Derek 4. Ray Milland 5. Gene
Wilder 6. Kevin Spacey 7. Stan Laurel 8. Rock Hudson 9. Brigitte Bardot
10. Mary Pickford

QUIZ 135

1 Which movie star, who played the Bond girl Solitaire, was born Joyce Frankenberg?

2 Who played Lois Lane on TV and the Bond girl Paris Carver in Tomorrow Never Dies?

3 In which film did Lois Chiles play a NASA astronaut called Holly Goodhead?

4 Who played the role of Tracy Draco in On Her Majesty's Secret Service?

5 What colour was the bikini worn by Ursula Andress in Dr No?

6 Which Swedish born actress played Mary Goodnight in The Man With The Golden Gun?

7 Who was the only woman in the 20th century to play the title role in a Bond movie?

8 Who played Pussy Galore in Goldfinger?

9 In which film did James Bond kill Elektra King?

10 Who was the first woman to sing a Bond theme?

ANSWERS

1. Jane Seymour 2. Teri Hatcher 3. Moonraker 4. Diana Rigg 5. White
6. Britt Ekland 7. Maud Adams in Octopussy 8. Honor Blackman 9. The World Is Not Enough 10. Shirley Bassey

QUIZ 136

• •

1 Which actor made his directorial debut with the 1997 film *Nil By Mouth*?

2 Which actor had hit records in 1987 with the songs, 'Respect Yourself' and 'Under The Boardwalk'?

3 In which musical did Gene Kelly and Frank Sinatra sing 'We Hate To Leave'?

4 Which director links the films *Hulk* and *Crouching Tiger Hidden Dragon*?

5 In which 2003 comedy did Steve Martin play the role of Tom Baker, the head of a family of twelve?

6 Which Canadian actress plays the role of Rogue in the *X Men* movies?

7 Was Richard Burton born in England, Ireland, Scotland or Wales?

8 Who played the title role in the 1988 film *Beetlejuice*?

9 In which 2003 comedy did Jack Nicholson fall in love with Diane Keaton?

10 Which Baron has been played on film by Kenneth Branagh, Sting and Peter Cushing?

ANSWERS

1. Gary Oldman 2. Bruce Willis 3. Anchors Aweigh 4. Ang Lee 5. *Cheaper By The Dozen* 6. Anna Paquin 7. Wales 8. Michael Keaton 9. *Something's Gotta Give* 10. Baron Frankenstein

QUIZ 137

• •

1 Who connects the 21st century films *Pearl Harbor*, *Black Hawk Down* and *40 Days And 40 Nights*?

2 Which detective solved the murder in the 1978 film *Death On The Nile*?

3 Who is the movie star sister of the singer Lorna Luft?

4 In 1947 who became the youngest ever actor to receive a knighthood?

5 In which 1999 romantic comedy did a film star called Anna Scott fall in love with a book shop owner called William Thacker?

6 Who did Steve McQueen marry in 1973 and divorce in 1978?

7 Who plays the role of Basil Exposition in the Austin Powers movies?

8 Who wrote a 1975 autobiography entitled Bring On The Empty Horses, eight years before his death?

9 Which 2003 animated movie features the voices of Brad Pitt, Michelle Pfeiffer and Catherine Zeta Jones?

10 In which 1991 movie remake did Nick Nolte play the husband of Jessica Lange?

ANSWERS

1. Josh Harnett 2. Hercule Poirot 3. Liza Minnelli 4. Laurence Olivier
5. *Notting Hill* 6. Ali McGraw 7. Michael York 8. David Niven
9. *Sinbad:Legend Of The Seven Seas* 10. *Cape Fear*

QUIZ 138

• •

1 Who played the bride to be of Billy Crystal in the comedy film Analyze This?

2 Who played Mel Gibson's leading lady in *What Women Want*?

3 Which wife of Charles Bronson played his leading lady in several films including the 1987 thriller Assassination?

4 Who played an ape called Ari in the 2001 film Planet Of The Apes?

5 In which film did Sandra Bullock play an FBI agent called Gracie Hart?

6 In 1992 which US President presented Audrey Hepburn with the Presidential Medal Of Freedom?

7 Which movie star was born Diane Hall in 1946?

8 Which star of the film *Thoroughly Modern Millie* was created a Dame Commander of the British Empire in 2000?

9 Who is the father of the movie star Drew Barrymore?

10 Who paid homage to Ursula Andress when emerging from the sea in a bikini in the Bond movie *Die Another Day*?

ANSWERS

1. Lisa Kudrow 2. Helen Hunt 3. Jill Ireland 4. Helena Bonham Carter
5. *Miss Congeniality* 6. George Bush Snr 7. Diane Keaton 8. Julie Andrews
9. John Barrymore Jnr 10. Halle Berry

QUIZ 139

• •

Which female movie star links each group of three film
   roles?

1   Lady Marian, Holly Golightly and Eliza Doolittle

2   Queen Victoria, Molly Brown and Dolores
     Claiborne

3   Helen of Troy, Velvet Brown and Cleopatra

4   Wendy Darling, Desdemona and Jean Brodie

5   Elizabeth I, Catherine the Great and Baby Jane
     Hudson

6   Carrie White, Alice Glover and Loretta Lynn

7   Stevie Smith, Elizabeth I and Lady Hamilton

8   Madam Rosmerta, Lara Antipova and Bathsheba
     Everdene

9   Anna Karenina, Scarlett O'Hara and Blanche
     DuBois

10   Natalie Cook, Jenny Everdeane and Mary Jensen

ANSWERS

1. Audrey Hepburn 2. Kathy Bates 3. Elizabeth Taylor 4. Maggie Smith
5. Bette Davis 6. Sissy Spacek 7. Glenda Jackson 8. Julie Christie 9. Vivien
Leigh 10. Cameron Diaz

QUIZ 140

1 Brody, Hooper and Quint were the three main characters in which film?

2 Who played Wanda Gershwitz in the 1988 film A Fish Called Wanda?

3 Which star of the film Goodfellas has a surname that is the plural for fish in the Italian language?

4 In which 2001 film did John Travolta play the villian of the piece Gabriel Shear?

5 Which 2003 animation features the characters of Marlin, Bloat and Bubbles?

6 In which 1965 Bond movie did Sean Connery come face to face with a shark?

7 In which 1987 cult movie did Richard E Grant utter the line, "Don't threaten me with a dead fish"?

8 What is the name of the goldfish in Pinocchio?

9 In which Oscar nominated film of 2003 did Ewan McGregor play the role of Ed Bloom?

10 Who played the role of Miranda Frost in the Bond movie Die Another Day?

ANSWERS

1. *Jaws* 2. Jamie Lee Curtis 3. Joe Pesci 4. *Swordfish* 5. *Finding Nemo*
6. *Thunderball* 7. *Withnail And I* 8. Cleo 9. *Big Fish* 10. Rosamund Pike

QUIZ 141

- -

1 Which film star was the subject of a controverisal biography entitled Mommie Dearest?

2 In which 1983 film did Jack Nicholson play a retired astronaut called Garrett Breedlove?

3 Which film septet were led by a gunslinger called Chris Adams?

4 Who played Inspector Steve Keller in the TV series The Streets Of San Francisco, before finding fame as a movie star?

5 Reloaded and Revolutions are the sub-titles of the sequels to which 1999 futuristic thriller?

6 Which war did the film character of Forrest Gump fight in ?

7 What animals are central to the plot in the 2004 animated movie Tusker?

8 Who was the oldest of the Marx Brothers?

9 In which 1949 film did Spencer Tracy and Katharine Hepburn play husband and wife attorneys called Adam and Amanda Bonner?

10 Who played the leading lady in the films Wildcats, Overboard and Deceived?

ANSWERS

1. Joan Crawford 2. *Terms Of Endearment* 3. *The Magnificent Seven*
4. Michael Douglas 5. *The Matrix* 6. Vietnam War 7. Elephants 8. Chico Marx
9. Adam's Rib 10. Goldie Hawn

QUIZ 142

. . . .

1 Who played Professor Trelawney in Harry Potter and the Prisoner of Azkaban?

2 In which 1998 film did Brenda Blethyn play the mother of Jane Horrocks?

3 For which 1956 film did Yul Brynner shave off all his hair?

4 Which Italian born film star once said, "Everything I have I owe to spaghetti"?

5 In which decade was Marlon Brando born?

6 In which 1995 film did Julianne Moore play the pregnant girlfriend of Hugh Grant?

7 Which movie icon is associated with the quote, "Anyone who hates small dogs and children can't be all bad"?

8 Who played the wife of Woody Allen in the 1991 film Scenes From A Mall?

9 Which Hitchcock thriller was the first major movie to feature a scene showing a flushing toilet?

10 Which movie star links the films The Rock, Snake Eyes and Wild At Heart?

ANSWERS

1. Emma Thompson 2. *Little Voice* 3. *The King And I* 4. Sophia Loren
5. 1920s 6. *Nine Months* 7. WC Fields 8. Bette Midler 9. *Psycho*
10. Nicholas Cage

QUIZ 143

• •

1 What is the sub-title of the film sequel Arthur 2?

2 Living Free was a sequel to which 1966 film starring Virginia McKenna?

3 What was the title of the 1990 sequel to 48 Hours?

4 Which sequel to The Hustler was released twenty-five years after the original?

5 The Return Of Jafar is a sequel to which Disney animated film?

6 Who played a big game hunter called Roland Tembo in the 1997 film sequel *Jurassic Park: The Lost World*?

7 Which 2004 film sequel is sub-titled *The Edge Of Reason*?

8 In which 1989 sequel did Sigourney Weaver reprise her role of Dana Barrett?

9 What was the title of the 1996 sequel to *Escape From New York*?

10 Which star of the TV sitcom Roseanne voiced Baloo the Bear in *The Jungle Book 2*?

ANSWERS

1. *On The Rocks* 2. *Born Free* 3. *Another 48 Hours* 4. *The Color Of Money*
5. *Aladdin* 6. Pete Postlethwaite 7. *Bridget Jones's Diary* 8. *Ghostbusters II*
9. *Escape From LA* 10. John Goodman

QUIZ 144

Which male movie star links each group of three film roles?

1 Marc Antony, Thomas Becket and Henry VIII

2 Fred Kite, Dr Strangelove and Fu Manchu

3 Pablo Picasso, Zorro and Dr John Harvey Kellogg

4 King Louis XVIII, Long John Silver and Harry Lime

5 Ernest Hemingway, Robin and D'Artagnan

6 Merlin, Harry Flashman and Caligula

7 Genghis Khan, Chisum and Colonel Mike Kirby

8 King Arthur, Robin Hood and Professor Henry Jones

9 Will Penny, Cardinal Richelieu and Moses

10 Steve Biko, Don Pedro of Aragon and Malcolm X

ANSWERS

1. Richard Burton 2. Peter Sellers 3. Anthony Hopkins 4. Orson Welles
5. Chris O'Donnell 6. Malcolm McDowell 7. John Wayne 8. Sean Connery
9. Charlton Heston 10. Denzel Washington

QUIZ 145

1. In which 1967 film did Richard Harris play King Arthur?

2. Which law man was portrayed by Henry Fonda in the movie western *My Darling Clementine*?

3. In 1925, who became the first actor to appear on the front cover of *Time Magazine*?

4. In which century was the film *Anne Of A Thousand Days* set?

5. In which 1998 film did Leonardo Di Caprio play King Louis XIV?

6. Which general was portrayed by Charlton Heston in Khartoum?

7. Which film starring John Wayne, was set in the 19th century, and featured the song 'The Green Leaves Of Summer'?

8. Which role did James Mason play in the 1953 film version of Julius Caesar?

9. In what year was the Oscar winning movie *Titanic* chiefly set?

10. In which 1981 film did Nigel Terry play the role of King Arthur?

ANSWERS

1. *Camelot* 2. Wyatt Earp 3. Charlie Chaplin 4. 16th 5. *The Man In The Iron Mask* 6. General Gordon 7. *The Alamo* 8. Brutus 9. 1912 10. *Excalibur*

QUIZ 146

• •

1   The song 'Call Me' by Blondie was the theme for which film starring Richard Gere?

2   Which cartoon character was brought to life on the big screen by Mark Addy and John Goodman?

3   Who did Kenneth Branagh marry in 1989 and divorce in 1995?

4   Who directed the 2001 remake of Ocean's Eleven?

5   What was the name of the doctor portrayed by Dirk Bogarde in a series of comedy films including *Doctor At Large*?

6   Which star of the film *Trading Places* holds the title of Lady Haden Guest?

7   In which classic movie did James Cagney play a sadistic gang leader called Cody Jarrett?

8   Which actress proclaimed, "I'm your number one fan" to James Caan in the film *Misery*?

9   Who played the brother of Dan Aykroyd in the 1980 film *The Blues Brothers*?

10 Who is the film star daughter of the actress Maureen O'Sullivan?

ANSWERS

1. American Gigolo 2. Fred Flintstone 3. Emma Thompson 4. Steven Soderbergh 5. Simon Sparrow 6. Jamie Lee Curtis 7. *White Heat* 8. Kathy Bates 9. John Belushi 10. Mia Farrow

QUIZ 147

. . . .

1 Who starred in and directed the film *Bananas*?

2 Which husband and wife connect the films *The Sound Of Music* and *The Pink Panther*?

3 Which 1997 comedy starred Jim Carrey as the head of the Reede family?

4 Who plays the title role in the 2004 action movie *Catwoman*?

5 Which movie star is mentioned in the lyrics of the pop songs 'We Didn't Start The Fire' and 'Wake Me Up Before You Go Go'?

6 Which Dame was awarded with The Fellowship Of The British Academy in 2002?

7 How many of the seven dwarfs wore glasses?

8 Who played the role of Satan in the 2000 film comedy *Little Nicky*?

9 Which actor has voiced characters in *Stuart Little* and *Homeward Bound*?

10 Which star of the *Superman* movies was seriously injured in a horse riding accident in 1995?

ANSWERS

1. Woody Allen 2. Julie Andrews and *Pink Panther* director Blake Edwards
3. Liar Liar 4. Halle Berry 5. Doris Day 6. Judi Dench 7. One – Doc 8. Harvey Keitel 9. Michael J Fox 10. Christopher Reeve

QUIZ 148

· ·

1 Which NM was portrayed by Morgan Freeman in the film *The Long Walk To Freedom*?

2 Which FP was the last film directed by Alfred Hitchcock?

3 What N is the name of the spacecraft in the sci-fi thriller Alien?

4 Which A was the goddess portrayed by Ursula Andress in the film *Clash Of The Titans*?

5 Which RZ directed the film *Forrest Gump*?

6 Which RW founded his own film production company called Blue Wolf Productions?

7 Which LM links the films *The Killers*, *Cat Ballou* and *The Delta Force*?

8 Which VH is portrayed by Hugh Jackman in a 2004 gothic horror?

9 Which GF was born George Booth?

10 Which PK played the leading lady of Mel Gibson in *Lethal Weapon II*?

ANSWERS

QUIZ 149

• •

1   What BP is the name of the pirate ship in the film *Pirates Of The Caribbean*?

2   Which JC voiced the character of Wilbur in the film *The Rescuers Down Under*?

3   What EC did Dorothy Gale travel to, to meet the Wizard of Oz?

4   Which FC was portrayed by Hugh Grant in the film Impromptu?

5   Which WS was portrayed by Christian Slater in *Robin Hood, Prince Of Thieves*?

6   Which LB is the father of the actor Jeff Bridges?

7   What BB is the name given to the gaffer's chief assistant on a film set?

8   Which JB was the third movie directed by Quentin Tarantino?

9   Which RR directed the films *When Harry Met Sally*, Misery and *A Few Good Men*?

10 Which MCD played a death row convict in the 1999 film *The Green Mile*?

ANSWERS

QUIZ 150

• •

1   Which duo had their last screen appearance together in a 1951 film entitled *Atoll K*?

2   Which iconic child star of the films *Bright Eyes* and *Heidi* retired from movie making in 1949?

3   Which movie legend made his last screen appearance in the 1956 film *The Harder They Fall* playing the role of Eddie Willis?

4   Who made his final screen appearance in the film *The Killers* before concentrating on his political career?

5   Who narrated the 2000 film *The Legend Of Bagger Vance*, the year before his death?

6   *High Society* was the last film of which movie star before she became a princess?

7   Which actor nicknamed The King Of Hollywood made his screen farewell in *The Misfits*?

8   The 1986 movie *Biggles* was the last film of which actor famed for Hammer horror movies?

9   Who moved on to a career in politics after she announced her retirement from acting following the 1993 film *King Of The Wind*?

10 Which *Carry On* star born George Hartree died in 1988?

ANSWERS

1. Laurel And Hardy 2. Shirley Temple 3. Humphrey Bogart 4. Ronald Reagan 5. Jack Lemmon 6. Grace Kelly 7. Clark Gable 8. Peter Cushing 9. Glenda Jackson 10. Charles Hawtrey

QUIZ 151

- -

Identify the films from their closing lines

1 It wasn't the planes, it was beauty killed the beast

2 Rosebud

3 Mr DeMille, I'm ready for my close up

4 A man's gotta know his limitations

5 After all tomorrow is another day

6 Killing generals could get to be a habit with me

7 Why she wouldn't even harm a fly

8 Louis, I think this is the beginning of a beautiful friendship

9 I do wish we could talk longer, but I'm having an old friend for dinner

10 Oh Auntie Em, there's no place like home

ANSWERS

1. *King Kong* 2. *Citizen Kane* 3. *Sunset Boulevard* 4. *Magnum Force* 5. *Gone With The Wind* 6. *The Dirty Dozen* 7. *Psycho* 8. *Casablanca* 9. *Silence Of The Lambs* 10. *The Wizard Of Oz*

QUIZ 152

1. In which movie does Tom Hanks play a prison guard called Paul Edgecomb?

2. Who has played the Prince of Wales, Charlie Chan and Hercule Poirot?

3. Which sport or pastime features in the 2003 film, *Touching The Void*?

4. Which heart-throb actor plays the father of the spy kids in the movie of the same name?

5. Who plays the role of Mark Darcy in the Bridget Jones movies?

6. What was Billy Crystal's profession in the comedy *Analyze This*?

7. Which boxer of yesteryear is portrayed by Russell Crowe in the film, *The Cinderella Man*?

8. What is the title of the third in the series of Austin Powers movies?

9. Which 1964 movie tells the story of an 1879 battle fought in Africa?

10. Which medieval author was portrayed by Paul Bettany in the movie *The Knight's Tale*?

ANSWERS

1. *The Green Mile* 2. Peter Ustinov 3. Mountaineering 4. Antonio Banderas
5. Colin Firth 6. Psychiatrist 7. Jim Braddock 8. *Goldmember* 9. Zulu
10. Geoffrey Chaucer

QUIZ 153

• •

1   In which movie did Steven Spielberg direct Richard Dreyfuss for the second time?

2   What is the name of the director brother of Ridley Scott?

3   Who starred in the movie 10 Rillington Place and directed Young Winston?

4   Who earned a Best Director Oscar for the movie The Deer Hunter?

5   Name the movie directed by Ken Loach in which a boy befriends a wild bird.

6   Name the director who wrote, directed and produced 2001: A Space Odyssey.

7   Who won a Best Director Oscar for the movie Platoon?

8   Which ancient hero does Sean Bean play in the 2004 historical epic, *Troy*?

9   Which star's list of credits as a director includes Quiz Show and Ordinary People?

10 A Passage to India was the last movie by which knighted British director?

ANSWERS

1. *Close Encounters of the Third Kind* 2. Tony Scott 3. Richard Attenborough
4. Michael Cimino 5. *Kes* 6. Stanley Kubrick 7. Oliver Stone 8. Odysseus
9. Robert Redford 10. Sir David Lean

QUIZ 154

. . . .

1 What item of attire did the Bond villain Oddjob use as a lethal weapon?

2 Which Bond movie features 'baddies' called Miranda Frost, Zao and Colonel Moon?

3 In which movie did 007 kill an agent called Red Grant aboard a train?

4 Who made her last appearance as Miss Moneypenny in *A View to a Kill*?

5 Hugo Drax was the villain in which Bond movie?

6 Who sang the theme song for *Thunderball*?

7 On which Caribbean island did Ian Fleming write the James Bond novels?

8 In which movie did the Israeli actor Topol play a Greek smuggler called Columbo?

9 The title of which Bond movie is also James Bond's family motto?

10 Which Scottish actor played a gangland boss called Valentin Zukovsky in two movies?

ANSWERS

1. A bowler hat 2. *Die Another Day* 3. *From Russia with Love* 4. Lois Maxwell
5. *Moonraker* 6. Tom Jones 7. Jamaica 8. *For Your Eyes Only*
9. *The World is Not Enough* 10. Robbie Coltrane

QUIZ 155

1 Which historical figure did Richard Widmark play in the *The Alamo*?

2 In which 1952 classic western did Gary Cooper star as Will Kane?

3 Chris, Vin, Bernardo, Lee, Harry, Britt and Chico are collectively known as who?

4 In which comedy western did Kevin Kline play dual roles?

5 Name Emilio Estevez's brother who co-starred with him in the movie *Young Guns*.

6 In which spoof western directed by Mel Brooks did Gene Wilder play the Waco Kid?

7 Who played Liberty Valance in *The Man Who Shot Liberty Valance*?

8 In which movie did Alan Ladd proclaim,"A man's gotta do what a man's gotta do"?

9 Kurt Russell played the lawman Wyatt Earp in which movie western?

10 Who played Mel Gibson's father in the comedy western Maverick?

ANSWERS

1. Jim Bowie 2. *High Noon* 3. *The Magnificent Seven* 4. Wild, Wild West
5. Charlie Sheen 6. *Blazing Saddles* 7. Lee Marvin 8. Shane 9. Tombstone
10. James Garner

QUIZ 156

. . . .

In which years were the following movies made?

1 *Dirty Dancing, Fatal Attraction* and *Wall Street*

2 *Gladiator, Mission Impossible II* and *The Perfect Storm*

3 *Cool Hand Luke, The Graduate* and *The Dirty Dozen*

4 *Shampoo, Jaws* and *Monty Python and The Holy Grail*

5 *The Hunt For Red October, Pretty Woman* and *Goodfellas*

6 *Lady and the Tramp, Rebel Without a Cause* and *The Seven Year Itch*

7 *Raiders of the Lost Ark, Arthur* and *Chariots of Fire*

8 *The Lion King, Speed* and *True Lies*

9 *Love Story, Patton* and *Woodstock*

10 *Jerry Maguire, Scream* and *Trainspotting*

ANSWERS

1. 1987 2. 2000 3. 1967 4. 1975 5. 1990 6. 1955 7. 1981 8. 1994 9. 1970 10. 1996

QUIZ 157

• •

Name that movie:

1 1968 – Steve McQueen, Faye Dunaway, Yaphet Kotto and Paul Burke

2 1993 – Robert Redford, Woody Harrelson, Demi Moore and Billy Connolly

3 1991 – Kevin Costner, Gary Oldman, Joe Pesci and John Candy

4 1993 – Sylvester Stallone, Wesley Snipes, Sandra Bullock and Nigel Hawthorne

5 1956 – Charlton Heston, Yul Brynner, Vincent Price and Edward G. Robinson

6 1959 – Tony Curtis, Jack Lemmon, Marilyn Monroe and George Raft

7 1995 – Johnny Depp, Christina Ricci, Michael Gambon and Christopher Lee

8 1945 – Elizabeth Taylor, Mickey Rooney, Donald Crisp and Angela Lansbury

9 1964 – Julie Andrews, Dick Van Dyke, David Tomlinson and Glynis Johns

10 1996 – Geoffrey Rush, John Gielgud, Lynn Redgrave and Googie Withers

ANSWERS

1. *The Thomas Crown Affair* 2. *Indecent Proposal* 3. *JFK* 4. *Demolition Man*
5. *The Ten Commandments* 6. *Some Like It Hot* 7. *Sleepy Hollow* 8. *National Velvet* 9. *Mary Poppins* 10. *Shine*

QUIZ 158

- -

1   *Return to Neverland* was a belated sequel to which Disney classic?

2   In the movie Gremlins which Disney picture did the gremlins watch in a cinema?

3   Which movie features the song 'I've got no Strings'?

4   Who did Demi Moore voice in the movie *The Hunchback of Notre Dame*?

5   Which classic novel was the subject of Disney's first live action feature in 1950?

6   In what year did Walt Disney die?

7   Musafa is the ruler of Pride Rock in which Disney animation?

8   Which Disney movie features the characters of Trixie, Henry, Zeb, Fred and Ted?

9   Which Disney movie features a crab called Sebastian?

10 The song 'You'll be in my Heart' won a Best Song Oscar for which Disney movie?

ANSWERS

1. *Peter Pan* 2. *Snow White and the Seven Dwarfs* 3. *Pinocchio*
4. Esmerelda 5. *Treasure Island* 6. 1966 7. *The Lion King* 8. *The Country Bears* 9. *The Little Mermaid* 10. *Tarzan*

QUIZ 159

. . . .

1 What kind of creature is Chewbacca?

2 Who was the apprentice of the Jedi knight Qui-Gon Jinn?

3 Which small furry forest dwellers live on Endor?

4 What is the title of the fifth movie to be made in the *Star Wars* series?

5 What is the name of the slug gangster that froze Han Solo in *The Empire Strikes Back*?

6 Which revered Jedi master spent his final years living on the planet of Dagobah?

7 Luke Skywalker lived on which planet before becoming a Jedi knight?

8 Organa is the last name of which *Star Wars* character?

9 What was Darth Vader called before he turned to the dark side?

10 Which actor voiced Darth Vader in *Star Wars*?

ANSWERS

1. Wookie 2. Obi-WanKenobi 3. Ewoks 4. Attack of the Clones 5. Jabba the Hutt 6. Yoda 7. Tatooine 8. Princess Leia 9. Anakin Skywalker
10. James Earl Jones

QUIZ 160

• •

1 Who starred in the 1927 movie *The Jazz Singer*?

2 Which silent movie star has a statue in Leicester Square, London?

3 What was the first name of the comedy actor "Fatty" Arbuckle?

4 Which legendary screen lover starred in *The Sheik and The Eagle*?

5 Which silent movie star was dubbed "Great Stone Face" as he never smiled on screen?

6 What were early cinemas called in the U.S.A., because the entry fee was five cents?

7 Which manic police force made their screen debut in a 1912 movie Hoffmeyer's Legacy?

8 What is the sub-title of a 2004 remake of *Dirty Dancing*?

9 Who plays the role of Davy Crockett in the 2004 remake of *The Alamo*?

10 In what decade were the Oscars first awarded?

ANSWERS

1. Al Jolson 2. Charlie Chaplin 3. Roscoe 4. Rudolph Valentino 5. Buster Keaton 6. Nickelodeon 7. *The KeystoneKops* 8. *Dirty Dancing: Havana Nights* 9. Billy Bob Thornton 10. 1920s

QUIZ 161

• •

1 Which 2002 movie sees David Arquette battling against giant spiders?

2 In *The Shining* Jack Nicholson fell into madness while staying at which hotel?

3 What type of creature eats its way through the cast in the 1999 movie *Lake Placid*?

4 Which serial killer was featured in the 1974 movie *The Texas Chainsaw Massacre*?

5 When Gary Oldman played Count Dracula, who played Van Helsing?

6 Name the actor who played Freddie Krueger in the Nightmare On Elm Street movies.

7 Michael Myers is the name of the killer in which series of horror movies?

8 Which star of the TV sitcom Friends played reporter Gale Weathers in the Scream movies?

9 Who has been played on screen by Kenneth Branagh and Peter Cushing?

10 Who played Rosemary in the movie Rosemary's Baby?

ANSWERS

1. *Eight Legged Freaks* 2. Overlook Hotel 3. Crocodile 4. Ed Gein
5. Anthony Hopkins 6. Robert Englund 7. *Halloween* 8. Courtney Cox
9. Baron Frankenstein 10. Mia Farrow

QUIZ 162

. . . .

1 Are *E.T.*'s eyes green, blue, brown or yellow?

2 Which animated duo are particularly fond of Wensleydale cheese?

3 In the movie *Home Alone* what is the first name of the boy left home alone?

4 What kind of animal is Rocky in *The Adventures of Rocky and Bullwinkle*?

5 Which two languages provide the dialogue of the controversial Mel Gibson directed movie, *The Passion Of The Christ*?

6 Who plays the partner of Owen Wilson in the 2004 movie version of *Starsky And Hutch*?

7 Which 2000 animated movie sees Emperor Kuzco transformed into a llama?

8 In the movie *Dinosaur* what is the name of the leader of the dinosaurs?

9 Is the family cat in the movie *Stuart Little*, black, white or tortoiseshell?

10 In which movie is Bugs Bunny assisted by basketball superstar Michael Jordan?

ANSWERS

1. Blue 2. Wallace and Gromit 3. Kevin 4. Squirrel 5. Latin and Aramaic
6. Ben Stiller 7. *The Emperor's New Groove* 8. Kron 9. White 10. *Space Jam*

QUIZ 163

• •

1. In which movie does a sheep dog called Fly become a foster parent to a pig?

2. What type of animal was voiced by Eddie Murphy in the movie *Shrek*?

3. Who stole Christmas in a 2000 movie?

4. In the movie Johnny Neutron what piece of kitchen equipment is made into a satellite?

5. What kind of animal is Bullwinkle in *The Adventures of Rocky and Bullwinkle*?

6. What is the name of Sid's dog in *Toy Story*?

7. Which movie features a hen called Ginger and farm owners called Mr. and Mrs. Tweedy?

8. In the movie *A Bug's Life* Flik hires circus performers to defend his colony from what?

9. Manfred, Sid and Diego are all characters in which movie?

10. What's the name of the bear who befriends Mowgli in *The Jungle Book*?

ANSWERS

1. *Babe* 2. Donkey 3. *The Grinch* 4. Toaster 5. Moose 6. Scud 7. *Chicken Run* 8. Grasshoppers 9. *Ice Age* 10. Baloo

QUIZ 164

1. Which actor plays Agent K in the Men in Black movies?

2. Which horror movie legend played the abominable Dr. Phibes in two movies?

3. Which super villain is played by Willem Dafoe in the 2002 movie Spiderman?

4. Who played the heroic Condorman in the 1981 Disney production?

5. Which actress had a fatal attraction for Michael Douglas?

6. In which action thriller did the hero and villain exchange identities?

7. Which Irish actor played the devil in the movie End of Days?

8. Who played the father of Indiana Jones in Indiana Jones and the Last Crusade?

9. Which Bond villain was played by Joseph Wiseman?

10. Who played the title role in the 1984 movie Supergirl?

ANSWERS

1. Tommy Lee Jones 2. Vincent Price 3. The Green Goblin 4. Michael Crawford 5. Glenn Close 6. Face/Off 7. Gabriel Byrne 8. Sean Connery 9. Dr. No 10. Helen Slater

QUIZ 165

1 Who played Mel Gibson's partner in the *Lethal Weapon* movies?

2 Which Bond movie tells of a plot to rob Fort Knox?

3 Which 1989 movie starred Tom Hanks as a detective with a large dog for a partner?

4 Which 1963 criminal event was chronicled in the 1988 movie *Buster*?

5 In the animated sequel *Shrek 2*, which prince is voiced by Rupert Everett?

6 Which series of movies featured a wisecracking cop called Axel Foley?

7 Who played Detective Jack Cates in the movie *48 Hours*?

8 In which movie did Sylvester Stallone play the sheriff of a small New Jersey town?

9 In which country did Butch Cassidy and the Sundance Kid meet a violent death?

10 Who played opposite Sean Connery in the movie *Entrapment*?

ANSWERS

1. Danny Glover 2. Goldfinger 3. Turner and Hooch 4. The Great Train Robbery 5. Prince Charming 6. Beverly Hills Cop 7. Nick Nolte 8. Cop Land 9. Bolivia 10. Catherine Zeta Jones

QUIZ 166

• •

1   Which movie about an army DJ was based on the life of Adrian Cronauer?

2   Who refused an Oscar for his 1970 portrayal of General Patton?

3   Who played Private Ryan in the movie *Saving Private Ryan*?

4   In which movie did Burt Lancaster enjoy a steamy love scene with Deborah Kerr?

5   Which 1957 movie told the story of British soldiers forced to build a bridge?

6   Who played Sergeant Joe Enders in the 2002 film *Windtalkers*?

7   In which movie did Tom Cruise play Vietnam veteran Ron Kovic?

8   Set in the Korean War, which movie features the characters of Hotlips and Hawkeye?

9   On whose novel was the film *The War Of The Worlds* set?

10 Name the movie in which Mel Gibson and Robert Downey Jr. played a pair of pilots.

ANSWERS

1. *Good Morning Vietnam* 2. George C. Scott 3. Matt Damon 4. *From Here to Eternity* 5. *Bridge on the River Kwai* 6. Nicholas Cage 7. *Born on the Fourth of July* 8. *M*A*S*H* 9. H.G. Wells 10. *Air America*

QUIZ 167

• •

1. Which 1990 mafia movie told the story of a 'wiseguy' called Henry Hill?

2. Name either of the films in which Robert De Niro played the Mafia boss, Paul Vitti.

3. Which actor played the role of Sonny Corleone, Michael's brother?

4. In the movies, Johnny Fontane was said to have been inspired by which singer?

5. Which director, better known for his spaghetti westerns, directed the 1984 gangster epic, *Once Upon A Time In America*?

6. Which word beginning with M was omitted deliberately from the screenplay of the movies?

7. Which actor played Tom Hagen, the legal advisor to the Corleone family?

8. Which 20th century gangster was played by Christian Slater in the 1991 film *Mobsters*?

9. On whose novel was *The Godfather* based?

10. Who played the title role in the 1959 film, *Al Capone*?

ANSWERS

1.Goodfellas *2.Analyze This or Analyze That* 3. James Caan 4. Frank Sinatra
5. Sergio Leone 6. Mafia 7. Robert Duvall 8. Lucky Luciano 9. Mario Puzo
10. Rod Steiger

QUIZ 168

. . . .

1 Who played the boss of Julia Roberts in the movie *Erin Brockovich*?

2 The Palme d'Or is the top award at which movie festival?

3 Who played the role of Professor Xavier in the movie *X-Men*?

4 Which movie was set in Dublin and featured the song 'Mustang Sally'?

5 Who played Count Dracula for the last time in the movie *The Satanic Rites of Dracula*?

6 Which heavyweight boxing champion had a cameo role in the 2001 movie Ocean's Eleven?

7 Who played the title role in the movie *Edward Scissorhands*?

8 In which movie did Richard Attenborough play a millionaire called John Hammond?

9 Which movie star is the daughter of Tippi Hedren, and the ex-wife of Don Johnson?

10 Which song was performed by the cast at the beginning of the movie *Grease*?

ANSWERS

QUIZ 169

• •

1 Which British actor played the husband of Geena Davis in the movie Stuart Little?

2 In which movie was Samuel L. Jackson devoured by a super-intelligent shark?

3 In which blockbuster movie does Will Smith have the call sign of Eagle?

4 Who provided the voice of Jessica Rabbit in the movie *Who Framed Roger Rabbit*?

5 The character of Austin Powers featured in the video for which Madonna song?

6 The 2001 film *Iris* chronicled the life of which writer?

7 What natural disaster did Pierce Brosnan combat in the movie *Dante's Peak*?

8 Which 2004 film sequel features villains called The Creeper and Captain Cutler?

9 Who directed the 2002 film *Spiderman*?

10 Which British actor played Boromir in *The Lord of the Rings*?

ANSWERS

1. Hugh Laurie   2. Deep Blue Sea   3. Independence Day   4. Kathleen Turner
5. "Beautiful Stranger" 6. Iris Murdoch   7. A volcanic eruption
8. Scooby Doo 2: Monsters Unleashed   9. Sam Raimi   10. Sean Bean

QUIZ 170

• •

1　In which century was Fred Astaire born?

2　The song 'White Christmas' featured in which movie starring Astaire and Crosby?

3　What was the title of the 1936 movie in which Astaire played a sailor on shore leave?

4　What name was he born with?

5　Which movie features the song 'Dancing Cheek to Cheek'?

6　What is the name of Astaire's sister, who was also his first dancing partner?

7　In which movie did he receive an Oscar nomination for his role as a conman?

8　His first movie starring with Ginger Rogers was called Flying Down to where?

9　In the movie Easter Parade, Astaire played Don Hewes. Who played Hannah Brown?

10　In what year of the 1980s did Astaire die?

ANSWERS

1. 19th century –born in 1899 2. Holiday Inn 3. *Follow the Fleet*
4. Frederick Austerlitz 5. *Top Hat* 6. Adele 7. *The Towering Inferno* 8. Rio
9. Judy Garland 10. 1987

QUIZ 171

1 What was the first name of Judy Garland's character in The Wizard of Oz?

2 Which 1964 movie co-starring Judy chronicled the 1948 Nazi War Trials?

3 Which director was she married to from 1945 to 1961?

4 Which diminutive actor was Judy's co-star in ten movies from 1938 to 1948?

5 In which movie did Judy sing "The Trolley Song"?

6 What was the name given to Judy when she was born?

7 How many times did she marry?

8 In which 1954 movie did James Mason play Judy's alcoholic husband?

9 What is the name of her youngest daughter who also performs as a singer?

10 In what year of the 1960s did Judy die, a few weeks after her 47th birthday?

ANSWERS

1. Dorothy 2. Judgment at Nuremberg 3. Vincente Minnelli 4. Mickey Rooney 5. Meet Me in St. Louis 6. Frances Gumm 7. Five times 8. A Star is Born 9. Lorna Luft 10. 1969

QUIZ 172

. . . .

1   In which country was The Lord of the Rings trilogy filmed?

2   Which star of the sitcom Cheers featured in the movie Three Men and a Baby?

3   Which famous model played the leading lady in The Boy Friend?

4   In which 2004 film does Johnny Depp play the author of the novel *Peter Pan*?

5   Who links the movies Seven, Along Came a Spider and *The Shawshank Redemption*?

6   Which superstar singer played Breathless Mahoney in *Dick Tracy*?

7   What is the favourite food of the *Teenage Mutant Ninja Turtles*?

8   Which James Bond comedy co-starred David Niven, Peter Sellers and Woody Allen?

9   Which star of the TV series Star Trek: The Next Generation, directed the 2004 action blockbuster Thunderbirds?

10 Which 2004 disaster movie is advertised with the publicity blurb, "Whoever said, Tomorrow is another day, didn't check the weather"?

ANSWERS

1. New Zealand   2. Ted Danson   3. Twiggy   4. JM Barrie's Neverlands
5. Morgan Freeman   6. Madonna   7. Pizza   8. *Casino Royale*   9. Jonathan Frakes   10. *The Day After Tomorrow*

QUIZ 173

- -

1 Which British actor, who died in 2003, played the role of Cassius in *Gladiator*?

2 Which British comedy star played the title role in *The Parole Officer*?

3 In 2002 which Hollywood star announced he was suffering from Alzheimer's disease?

4 In which country was the critically acclaimed 2002 film *Rabbit Proof Fence* set?

5 Which actor was forced to take a lie detector test in the 2000 comedy Meet the Parents?

6 Which movie co-starring Robert Carlyle and Samuel L. Jackson is set in Liverpool?

7 Which actress links the films, *Love Actually*, *Pirates Of The Caribbean* and *Bend It Like Beckham*?

8 Who played the C.I.A. operative Jack Ryan in the 2002 movie *The Sum of all Fears*?

9 Who played the leading lady in *What Women Want* and *As Good as it Gets*?

10 Name the baby in the 2002 movie Monsters Inc.

ANSWERS

1. David Hemmings 2. Steve Coogan 3. Charlton Heston 4. Australia
5. Ben Stiller 6. The 51st State 7. Keira Knightley 8. Ben Affleck 9. Helen
Hunt 10. Boo

QUIZ 174

• •

1 Who played Rebecca Howe in the sitcom Cheers and Lieutenant Saavik in Star Trek II?

2 In which American city was the Ridley Scott sci-fi thriller Bladerunner set?

3 Which H.G. Wells novel was first filmed in 1960 starring Rod Taylor?

4 In which movie were senior citizens rejuvenated by extra-terrestrial powers?

5 Name the 1997 sci-fi action thriller that starred Bruce Willis and Gary Oldman.

6 In which movie were John Hurt and Sigourney Weaver crewmates aboard a spacecraft?

7 Who played the time traveller Dr. Emmett Brown in the *Back to the Future* movies?

8 Which droid spoke the first line of dialogue in the movie *Star Wars*?

9 Who plays the title role in the 2004 movie epic *King Arthur*?

10 In which movie did Jack Nicholson play President Dale?

ANSWERS

QUIZ 175

1 Who composed the music for the spaghetti western The Good, the Bad and the Ugly?

2 What are the first names of Rodgers & Hammerstein?

3 Which king of ragtime music featured in the Oscar-winning movie The Sting?

4 Who wrote the songs for the musical *Oliver*?

5 Which soundtrack featured Whitney Houston singing 'I'm Every Woman'?

6 Mike Oldfield's 'Tubular Bells' featured in which horror movie?

7 Which song performed by Tom Jones featured in the movie *The Full Monty*?

8 Which film featured the Madonna song 'Into The Groove' on the soundtrack?

9 Which trio sang six songs on the soundtrack for *Saturday Night Fever*?

10 Which Greek musician won an Oscar for his music in the movie *Chariots of Fire*?

ANSWERS

1. Ennio Morricone 2. Richard and Oscar 3. Scott Joplin 4. Lionel Bart
5. The Bodyguard 6. The Exorcist 7. 'You Can Leave Your Hat On'
8. Desperately Seeking Susan 9. The Bee Gees 10. Vangelis

QUIZ 176

• •

1 Which owner of a chocolate factory did Charlie Bucket meet on screen?

2 Which cartoon movie tells the story of a lost Russian princess?

3 Which American state shares its name with the first name of Dr. Jones?

4 What is the name of Tarzan's female companion?

5 What is the name of Disney's flying elephant?

6 Which capital city did the Rugrats venture to in a 2000 movie?

7 What does the A stand for in the Steven Spielberg movie A.I.?

8 What kind of animal is Maid Marian in Disney's cartoon version of Robin Hood?

9 What is the name of the young boy who is a close friend of Winnie the Pooh?

10 Which girl accompanied Peter Pan to Never Never Land?

ANSWERS

1. Willy Wonka   2. Anastasia   3. Indiana   4. Jane   5. Dumbo   6. Paris
7. Artificial   8. Fox   9. Christopher Robin   10. Wendy Darling

QUIZ 177

. . . .

1   In which country is the Disney movie *Mulan* set?

2   What kind of creepy crawlies featured in the movie *Arachnophobia*?

3   What kind of dinosaur is the monster featured in the 1998 movie *Godzilla*?

4   Robbie Williams sang 'We are the Champions' for which movie?

5   How many of the seven dwarfs have a name beginning with S?

6   In the 2002 animated movie what is the name of the stallion of the Cimarron?

7   What is the name of the bird that Stuart Little rescues from the clutches of a falcon?

8   Which 1997 cartoon film features the characters of Pain, Panic and Pegasus?

9   To which islands do the Spy Kids venture in their second film outing?

10 What is the name of Fred Flintstone's best friend?

ANSWERS

1. China   2. Spiders   3. Tyrannosaurus Rex   4. *A Knight's Tale*   5. Two – Sleepy and Sneezy   6. Spirit   7. Margalo   8. *Hercules*   9. Islands of Lost Dreams   10. Barney Rubble

QUIZ 178

• •

1   In which 1999 movie did Brendan Fraser play the all-action hero Rick O'Connell?

2   Which actor, who starred in *The Champ*, is the father of Angelina Jolie?

3   Who played the explorer Phileas Fogg in the 2004 film *Around The World In Eighty Days*?

4   In which movie does Sean Connery play a submarine commander?

5   In which horror movie did Gregory Peck and Lee Remick play Damien's parents?

6   Which 2003 Disney animation features bears called Koda and Kenai?

7   Which explorer was portrayed in the movie 1492: The Conquest of Paradise?

8   Whose 1987 autobiography is entitled *Also Known as Shirley*?

9   Which actor has played Batman, The Saint and Doc Holliday in movies?

10 In which city is the movie *Wall Street* set?

ANSWERS

1. *The Mummy*   2. Jon Voight   3. Steve Coogan   4. *The Hunt for Red October*
5. The Omen   6. *Brother Bear*   7. Christopher Columbus   8. Shelley Winters
9. Val Kilmer   10. New York

QUIZ 179

. . . .

1 In which 1995 movie did Susan Sarandon wear a wimple?

2 Which Icelandic pop star won a Best Actress award at the 2000 Cannes Film Festival?

3 Who was Oscar nominated for his roles in the films, *American History X* and *Primal Fear*?

4 In the movie *The Lavender Hill Mob*, gold bullion is made into models of what?

5 In which 2003 comedy did Eddie Murphy play the role of Charlie Hinton?

6 Which ex-husband of Barbra Streisand starred in *A Bridge Too Far*?

7 What number can precede Days In Tibet, Per Cent Solution and Year Itch, to give the titles of three films?

8 Which actor played Colonel Nathan R. Jessup in *A Few Good Men*?

9 Which character was described as "The Barbarian" and "The Destroyer"?

10 Name Adolf Hitler's henchman in the movie The Eagle Has Landed.

ANSWERS

1. *Dead Man Walking* 2. Bjork 3. Ed Norton 4. Eiffel Tower 5. *Daddy Day Care* 6. Elliot Gould 7. Seven 8. Jack Nicholson 9. Conan 10. Heinrich Himmler

QUIZ 180

. . . .

1. Which 1939 epic saw Olivia de Havilland playing Melanie Hamilton?

2. Which movie masterpiece tells the story of newspaper tycoon Charles Foster Kane?

3. Which movie features 'The Nutcracker Suite' and 'The Sorcerer's Apprentice'?

4. Which scientist and Nobel Prize winner was played by Greer Garson in a 1943 movie?

5. Which 2001 film saw Penelope Cruz and Cameron Diaz vying for the affections of Tom Cruise?

6. Which 1944 movie features a huge mansion called Thornfield Hall?

7. Which movie tells the tale of two old ladies who poison gentlemen callers at their home?

8. Where did Mr. Smith go to in a 1939 movie starring James Stewart?

9. Name the 1942 movie in which James Cagney plays a song and dance man.

10. In which movie did John Wayne play the Ringo Kid?

ANSWERS

1. *Gone With The Wind* 2. *Citizen Kane* 3. *Fantasia* 4. Marie Curie 5. *Vanilla Sky* 6. Jane Eyre 7. Arsenic and Old Lace 8. Washington 9. *Yankee Doodle Dandy* 10. *Stagecoach*

QUIZ 181

1 In which building did the murders take place in the movie *Psycho*?

2 On which mountain does the climax of the movie *North by Northwest* take place?

3 What is the title of the Hitchcock movie that featured the song 'Que Sera Sera'?

4 In which 1958 movie did James Stewart have a morbid fear of heights?

5 Which future princess starred in the movie Dial M for Murder?

6 In which movie does Melanie travel to Bodega Bay to meet a lawyer called Mitch?

7 Name the actor who played Professor Michael Armstrong in Torn Curtain.

8 Which mother and daughter connect the films, *Private Benjamin* and *Raising Helen*?

9 In which movie did Cary Grant play a jewel thief called John Robie?

10 What was Hitchcock's last movie as a director?

ANSWERS

1. Bates Motel 2. Mount Rushmore 3. *The Man who Knew too Much*
4. *Vertigo* 5. Grace Kelly 6. *The Birds* 7. Paul Newman 8. Goldie Hawn and Kate Hudson 9. *To Catch a Thief* 10. *Family Plot*

QUIZ 182

• •

The following are the real names of actors and movies they've starred in. Can you give the actors' stage names?

1 Caryn Johnson in *Ghost*

2 Joyce Frankenberg in *Live and Let Die*

3 Allen Konigsberg in *The Purple Rose of Cairo*

4 Jerome Silberman in *Blazing Saddles*

5 Camille Javal in *And God Created Woman*

6 Joseph Yule Jr. in *National Velvet*

7 Taidje Khan Jr. in *The Magnificent Seven*

8 Anna Maria Italiano in *The Graduate*

9 William Henry Pratt in *Frankenstein*

10 Bernard Schwartz in *The Vikings*

ANSWERS

1. Whoopi Goldberg 2. Jane Seymour 3. Woody Allen 4. Gene Wilder
5. Brigitte Bardot 6. Mickey Rooney 7. Yul Brynner 8. Anne Bancroft
9. Boris Karloff 10. Tony Curtis

QUIZ 183

Who...

1 Born 26 January 1925 in Cleveland, appeared in *The Towering Inferno*

2 Born 10 February 1930 in Detroit, appeared in *The Towering Inferno*

3 Born 10 August 1960 in Malaga, appeared in *Interview with the Vampire*

4 Born 31 August 1928 in Nebraska, appeared in *The Great Escape*

5 Born 22 February 1975 in Los Angeles, appeared in *Charlie's Angels*

6 Born 25 February 1969 in Swansea, appeared in *Traffic*

7 Born 14 August 1968 in Cleveland, appeared in *Monster's Ball*

8 Born 31 December 1937 in Port Talbot, appeared in *A Bridge Too Far*

9 Born 18 February 1954 in New Jersey, appeared in *Look Who's Talking*

10 Born 25 May 1939 in Burnley, appeared in *Lord of the Rings*

ANSWERS

1. Paul Newman   2. Robert Wagner   3. Antonio Banderas   4. James Coburn
5. Drew Barrymore   6. Catherine Zeta Jones   7. Halle Berry   8. Anthony
Hopkins   9. John Travolta   10. Ian McKellen

QUIZ 184

- -

1 In which 2000 movie did Richard Harris play Emperor Marcus Aurelius?

2 Who played an oil driller called Harry Stamper in the movie *Armageddon*?

3 Which decade did Marty McFly travel back to in the 1985 movie *Back to the Future*?

4 *Planet of the Apes* (2001) is a remake of a movie starring which Hollywood legend?

5 Who played William Rose Bailey in the action thriller *Charlie's Angels: Full Throttle*?

6 Neo, Trinity, Tank and Mouse are all characters in which 1999 movie?

7 What was the world's top box-office movie of the 1970s?

8 In which 1993 movie is Dr. Richard Kimble wrongly accused of murdering his wife?

9 Which 1996 movie saw Bill Paxton chasing tornadoes?

10 In which 2003 romantic comedy did Catherine Zeta Jones fall in love with George Clooney?

ANSWERS

1. *Gladiator* 2. Bruce Willis 3. The 1950s 4. Charlton Heston 5. Bruce Willis
6. *The Matrix* 7. *Star Wars* 8. *The Fugitive* 9. *Twister* 10. *Intolerable Cruelty*

QUIZ 185

. . . .

1. Which musical featured the song 'Matchmaker, Matchmaker'?

2. In which city is the 1972 musical *Cabaret* set?

3. What is the name of the rival gang of the Jets in *West Side Story*?

4. Which award-winning movie tells the story of a flower girl called Eliza Doolittle?

5. The song 'Luck be a Lady' was heard in which musical starring Frank Sinatra?

6. In which 2001 movie did Ewan McGregor play Christian?

7. Deborah Kerr sang 'Getting to Know You' to a group of children in which movie?

8. What is the title of the musical that tells the story of the Pontabee siblings?

9. Which 1986 box office flop saw Patsy Kensit singing the song ,'Having It All'?

10. Which 1979 movie was set at the New York School of Performing Arts?

ANSWERS

1. *Fiddler on the Roof* 2. Berlin 3. The Sharks 4. *My Fair Lady* 5. *Guys and Dolls* 6. *Moulin Rouge* 7. *The King and I* 8. *Seven Brides for Seven Brothers* 9. *Absolute Beginners* 10. *Fame*

QUIZ 186

1 What was the tagline for *Close Encounters of the Third Kind*?

2 Which 1993 blockbuster co-starred Laura Dern, Jeff Goldblum and Sam Neill?

3 Which movie earned Spielberg his first Oscar for Best Director?

4 In which European city is the 2002 Oscar winning movie *The Pianist* chiefly set?

5 What is the name of the boat skippered by Captain Quint in the movie *Jaws*?

6 What is the title of Spielberg's 1991 adaptation of the story of Peter Pan?

7 Name the leading lady in the Spielberg movie *Indiana Jones and the Temple of Doom*.

8 Which 2002 movie starring Tom Cruise is set in the year 2054?

9 In which movie does a gang of children search for the treasure of "One Eyed" Willy?

10 In what decade was Spielberg born?

ANSWERS

1."We are not alone" 2. *Jurassic Park* 3. *Schindler's List* 4. Warsaw 5. The Orca 6. *Hook* 7. Kate Capshaw 8. Minority Report 9. The Goonies 10. 1940s – born in 1946

QUIZ 187

• •

1 Jafar is the name of the villain in which 1992 Disney movie?

2 Name the movie in which Gene Kelly dances with Jerry from the Tom and Jerry cartoons.

3 Which actor links *The Flintstones*, *Ghostbusters* and *Honey I Shrunk the Kids*?

4 In which animation does the character of Richard Tyler meet Long John Silver?

5 Uncle Remus recounts the tales of Brer Rabbit and Brer Fox in which 1946 movie?

6 Which 1999 cartoon movie is subtitled Bigger, Longer and Uncut?

7 In 2002 the first Oscar for Best Animation went to which movie?

8 Who provided the voice of Mickey Mouse in his cartoon debut?

9 J. Worthington Foulfellow, Stromboli and Figaro are all characters in which movie?

10 Which movie tells the story of a Hawaiian girl who adopts a dog that is disguised as an alien?

ANSWERS

QUIZ 188

1 In which movie did Tom Hanks play a boy trapped in a 32-year-old man's body?

2 In the title of a 1999 movie, a dragon is hiding and what animal is crouching?

3 When Olivia de Havilland played Maid Marian, who played Robin Hood?

4 Who played Rita in Educating Rita?

5 Which movie star is the daughter of director John Huston?

6 In which 1990 movie did Julia Roberts and Kiefer Sutherland play medical students?

7 In which 1968 movie did Sally Anne Howes play Truly Scrumptious?

8 In which 1997 movie did Gaz, Gerald, Guy and Dave shed their clothes?

9 Which Scottish comedian played an auctioneer in Indecent Proposal?

10 In a 1993 version of The Three Musketeers who played D'Artagnan?

ANSWERS

1. Big 2. Tiger 3. Errol Flynn 4. Julie Walters 5. Angelica Huston
6. *Flatliners* 7. *Chitty Chitty Bang Bang* 8. *The Full Monty* 9. Billy Connolly
10. Chris O'Donnell

QUIZ 189

1 What is the name of the arch enemy of Austin Powers?

2 Which singer did Val Kilmer play in the 1991 movie The Doors?

3 Which movie starring Whoopi Goldberg is also the title of a Rolling Stones hit record?

4 Who did Rosie O'Donnell play in the 1994 movie *The Flintstones*?

5 In which 1997 movie did Mel Gibson play a paranoid character called Jerry Fletcher?

6 Which 1950 musical told the story of the wild west heroine Annie Oakley?

7 Jason Takes Manhattan is the sub-title of the 8th movie in which series of horror flicks?

8 In which 1993 movie does Kevin Kline impersonate the President of the U.S.A.?

9 In which movie does a weatherman have to live the same day over and over again?

10 Which 1998 movie saw Wesley Snipes vanquishing vampires?

ANSWERS

1. Dr. Evil 2. Jim Morrison 3. *Jumping Jack Flash* 4. Betty Rubble
5. *Conspiracy Theory* 6. *Annie Get Your Gun* 7. *Friday the 13th* 8. *Dave*
9. *Groundhog Day* 10. *Blade*

QUIZ 190

• •

1   In which 1988 movie did James Belushi play a narcotics cop who teamed up with a dog?

2   What was the title of the 1943 movie that saw the debut of Lassie?

3   Which screen cowboy of yesteryear rode a horse called "Topper"?

4   What breed of dog is Beethoven in the 1992 movie?

5   Which sequel features Lennie the weasel, Joey the raccoon and Archie the bear?

6   What was the name of Roy Rogers' dog?

7   Fiver and Hazel are the names of rabbits in which movie?

8   Which canine screen hero died in the arms of Jean Harlow?

9   In which 1971 Disney movie did a duck lay eggs with solid gold yolks?

10 In the 1972 movie Ben, is Ben a cat, a rat or a horse?

ANSWERS

1. K-9 2. Lassie Come Home 3. Hopalong Cassidy 4. St. Bernard 5. Dr Doolittle II 6. Bullet 7. Watership Down 8. Rin Tin Tin 9. Million Dollar Duck 10. Rat

QUIZ 191

1 In the 1974 movie *The Mean Machine*, who played a former pro-footballer Paul Crewe?

2 Which Z Cars actor won an Oscar for Best Screenplay for the movie *Chariots of Fire*?

3 What sport features in the 1993 movie *The Sandlot*?

4 The movie *When We Were Kings* chronicles Muhammad Ali's fight with which boxer?

5 What is the title of the 1986 movie in which Paul Newman plays a pool hustler?

6 Who kept goal for the allied team in *Escape to Victory*?

7 Who played golf pro Roy McAvoy in the 1996 movie *Tin Cup*?

8 What sport is featured in *Pharlap*, *Champions* and *The Shamrock Handicap*?

9 What number appears on the side of Herbie, the VW Beetle racing car in *The Love Bug*?

10 Who played Rod Tidwell, wide receiver for the Arizona Cardinals, in *Jerry Maguire*?

ANSWERS

1. Burt Reynolds 2. Colin Welland 3. Baseball 4. George Foreman 5. The Color of Money 6. Sylvester Stallone 7. Kevin Costner 8. Horseracing 9. 53 10. Cuba Gooding Jr.

QUIZ 192

1 What is Crocodile Dundee's first name?

2 To which U.S. city does Crocodile Dundee travel in the third movie of the series?

3 In which year was the first Crocodile Dundee movie made?

4 Who plays the role of Sue Charlton in the Crocodile Dundee movies?

5 What is the first name of Dundee's Australian sidekick played by John Meillon?

6 Which group had a hit with the song from Crocodile Dundee entitled "Live it Up"?

7 What is the name of Crocodile Dundee's hometown in Australia?

8 What is the name of Sue and Dundee's nine-year-old son in the third movie?

9 To which U.S. city did Dundee travel with Sue Charlton in the first movie?

10 What does Crocodile Dundee call women?

ANSWERS

1. Mick 2. Los Angeles 3. 1986 4. Linda Kozlowski 5. Wally 6. Mental as Anything 7. Walkabout Creek 8. Mikey 9. New York 10. Sheilas

QUIZ 193

1 Who had a hit with the theme song from the original *Ghostbusters* movie?

2 In which 1982 movie is a family's youngest daughter kidnapped by ghosts?

3 Who played Molly in the movie *Ghost*?

4 In which ghost story does Nicole Kidman star as the mother of two young children?

5 Who played the title role in Beetlejuice?

6 In which 1999 movie did Haley Joel Osment say, "I see dead people"?

7 In which ghost story were Harrison Ford and Michelle Pfeiffer haunted?

8 Who plays Dr. Raymond Stantz in *Ghostbusters*?

9 Which children's character is described as "The Friendly Ghost"?

10 In which movie does Margaret Rutherford play Madame Arcati?

ANSWERS

1. Robert Parker Jr. 2. *Poltergeist* 3. Demi Moore 4. The Others 5. Michael Keaton 6. *The Sixth Sense* 7. *What Lies Beneath* 8. Dan Aykroyd 9. Casper 10. *Blithe Spirit*

QUIZ 194

. . . .

1 Who played Chief Brody in the movie *Jaws*?

2 Which star of Bedtime for Bonzo went on to become a world leader?

3 Who plays the title role in the 2002 movie *The Bourne Identity*?

4 Which Scottish actor voiced a dragon called Draco in the movie *Dragonheart*?

5 Who died aged 36 shortly after making the movie *The Misfits*?

6 Which 2001 movie includes the surname of England's 2002 Football World Cup captain?

7 For which comedy western did Lee Marvin win an Oscar for playing twin brothers?

8 Which footballer connects the movies *Snatch*, *Swordfish* and *Gone in 60 Seconds*?

9 Which animator created Wallace and Gromit?

10 What is the title of the 1997 movie in which John Travolta plays an angel?

ANSWERS

1. Roy Scheider 2. Ronald Reagan 3. Matt Damon 4. Sean Connery
5. Marilyn Monroe 6. *Bend it Like Beckham* 7. Cat Ballou 8. Vinnie Jones
9. Nick Park 10. Michael

QUIZ 195

1 In which movie does Kevin Bacon discover the secret of invisibility?

2 What kind of shop was owned by Hugh Grant in Notting Hill?

3 In which country was Billy Hayes imprisoned in Midnight Express?

4 In what movie, an update of Cyrano de Bergerac, did Steve Martin play a firefighter?

5 Who did Buster Crabbe play on movie when he was battling against Ming the Merciless?

6 Who plays Professor Charles Xavier in the X Men action thrillers?

7 Who starred in the movie Clockwise as a headmaster called Mr. Stimpson?

8 Who played the police detective Officer Nordberg in Naked Gun?

9 What connects Crimson Tide, The Enemy Below and The Hunt for Red October?

10 In which movie did James Dean play the role of Jim Stark?

ANSWERS

1. *Hollow Man* 2. A bookshop 3. Turkey 4. Roxanne 5. Flash Gordon
6. Patrick Stewart 7. John Cleese 8. O.J. Simpson 9. Submarines 10. *Rebel Without A Cause*

QUIZ 196

• •

1 Which knighted actor played God in the comedy movie *Time Bandits*?

2 What was the first *Carry On* movie?

3 According to the title of a 1977 movie, what is the name of Dracula's dog?

4 The climax of *The Third Man* takes place in the sewers of which capital city?

5 In *When Harry Met Sally*, what is Harry's last name?

6 Who did Charlton Heston portray in *The Agony and the Ecstasy*?

7 Which 1981 Oscar-winning movie chronicles the life story of John Reed?

8 Who wore a cantilevered bra, specially designed for her in *The Outlaw*?

9 Which Disney character married Faline?

10 Who wrote the play *Still Life* on which the classic love story *Brief Encounter* is based?

ANSWERS

1. Sir Ralph Richardson 2. *Carry On Sergeant* 3. Zoltan 4. Vienna 5. Burns
6. Michelangelo 7. Reds 8. Jane Russell 9. *Bambi* 10. Sir Noel Coward

QUIZ 197

. . . .

1 The 1999 movie, *10 Things I Hate About You*, was based on which Shakespeare play?

2 In which 1997 film did Jack Nicholson appear alongside a dog called Verdell?

3 What was Edith Head listed as in over 300 movies from the 1930s to the 1980s?

4 Which movie starring Jane Fonda was based on a comic strip by Jean Claude Forest?

5 In which 2000 film did Helen Hunt play the character of Darcy McGuire who falls in love with the character of Nick Marshall, played by Mel Gibson?

6 Who played Inspector Clouseau in the 1968 movie entitled Inspector Clouseau?

7 The movie *The Music Lovers* was based on the life of which classical composer?

8 What was the title of the first sound movie that featured Mickey Mouse?

9 Which movie with Richard Burton was the first to be filmed in cinemascope?

10 In which 1995 movie did Sophie Marceau play Princess Isabelle?

ANSWERS

1. *The Taming of The Shrew* 2. *As Good As It Gets* 3. Costume designer
4. *Barbarella* 5. *What Women Want* 6. Alan Arkin 7. Tchaikovsky
8. *Steamboat Willie* 9. *The Robe* 10. *Braveheart*

QUIZ 198

• •

1 What is the name of the tomb raider played on screen by Angelina Jolie?

2 Which *Friends* actress is married to the movie star David Arquette?

3 Which man of steel is vulnerable when exposed to kryptonite?

4 In the movie *Grease*, does Danny fall in love with Sindy, Sandy or Mandy?

5 Which sport features in the movie The Bad News Bears?

6 Which star of the *Scream* horror movies and the TV series *Friends* gave birth to a baby daughter called Coco in 2004?

7 Who gains his strength from eating spinach?

8 Which movie is introduced with the words, "A long time ago in a galaxy far, far away"?

9 Which singer and actress married singer Marc Anthony in June 2004?

10 In which movie did Lindsay Lohan play twin sisters?

ANSWERS

1. Lara Croft 2. Courtney Cox Arquette 3. *Superman* 4. Sandy 5. Baseball
6. Courtney Cox Arquette 7. Popeye 8. *Star Wars* 9. Jennifer Lopez 10. *The Parent Trap*

QUIZ 199

• •

1   In which Disney movie does a spaniel fall in love with a mongrel?

2   The wrestler "The Rock" played which king in *The Mummy Returns*?

3   What type of creatures are Sam, Merry and Pippin in *The Lord of the Rings*?

4   What is the name of the evil lord in the movie *Shrek*?

5   Is the hero of the movie *Chicken Run* called Ricky, Stocky or Rocky?

6   What part of the body is the scarecrow searching for in *The Wizard of Oz*?

7   In which movie did an alien phone home with the help of Elliot?

8   In which movie did Robin Williams dress up as a nanny?

9   Which American wrestler appeared in the movies *Rocky III* and *Muppets From Space*?

10 In which animated movie does a captain fall in love with an American Indian princess?

ANSWERS

1. *Lady and the Tramp* 2. *The Scorpion King* 3. Hobbits 4. Lord Farquaad
5. *Rocky* 6. The brain 7. *E.T.* 8. *Mrs. Doubtfire* 9. Hulk Hogan 10. *Pocahontas*

QUIZ 200

. . . .

1 Who won consecutive Best Actor Oscars in the 1990s?

2 Which actress played Karen Silkwood, Lindy Chamberlain and Sarah Woodrough?

3 Which star of the TV sitcom Cheers played Dad in Getting Even With Dad?

4 In 2002, who became the youngest ever actor to win a Best Actor Oscar?

5 Who played Bridget Jones on screen?

6 Who was nominated for the Best Actor Oscar in 1995 for *Witness*?

7 Which actor played the detective Eddie Valiant in *Who Framed Roger Rabbit*?

8 Who made a tearful Oscar acceptance speech for her role in *Shakespeare in Love*?

9 Which mythical creature featured in the movie *Splash!*?

10 Which duo sang 'Trail of the Lonesome Pine' in Way Out West?

ANSWERS

1. Tom Hanks 2. Meryl Streep 3. Ted Danson 4. Adrien Brody 5. Renee Zellwegger 6. Harrison Ford 7. Bob Hoskins 8. Gwyneth Paltrow 9. Mermaid 10. Laurel and Hardy

QUIZ 201

- -

1 Which movie featured a pair of unlikely brothers called Julius and Vincent Benedict?

2 What is the family connection between *Easy Rider*, *Klute* and *Twelve Angry Men*?

3 In which heist movie did Steve McQueen star with his then wife Ali McGraw?

4 Which father of two movie actor sons starred in *Apocalypse Now*?

5 Name the actress mother of Mia Farrow, who starred in several *Tarzan* movies as Jane.

6 Which movie legend married Frank Sinatra, Mickey Rooney and Artie Shaw?

7 Name Warren Beatty's sister who starred in *Terms of Endearment*.

8 In which movie did Elizabeth Taylor first star with Richard Burton?

9 Which of the Baldwin brothers married Kim Basinger?

10 Who is the movie star mother of Carrie Fisher?

ANSWERS

1. Twins 2. The Fonda family 3. The Getaway 4. Martin Sheen 5. Maureen O'Sullivan 6. Ava Gardner 7. Shirley MacLaine 8. Cleopatra 9. Alec Baldwin 10. Debbie Reynolds

QUIZ 202

. . . .

1   Which 1995 movie was introduced by, "Five criminals, one line-up, no coincidence"?

2   Which character was Clint Eastwood playing when he said, "Go ahead, make my day"?

3   Which movie ended with the words, "Tomorrow is another day"?

4   Which movie contains the following line, "It's dark and we're wearing sunglasses"?

5   Which character is associated with the catchphrase, "To infinity and beyond"?

6   In which movie did Arnold Schwarzenegger first utter the line, "I'll be back"?

7   Which actor on screen said, "Do you think we used enough dynamite there Butch?"

8   In which movie did Michael Douglas say, 'Greed for lack of a better word is good'?

9   Which movie includes the line, "If you played it for her you can play it for me"?

10 In the 1949 movie *White Heat*, who said, "Made it ma! Top of the world!"?

ANSWERS

1. *The Usual Suspects* 2. Harry Callahan 3. *Gone With The Wind* 4. *The Blues Brothers* 5. Buzz Lightyear 6. *Terminator* 7. Robert Redford as Butch Cassidy 8. *Wall Street* 9. *Casablanca* 10. James Cagney

QUIZ 203

• •

1   What is added to a movie by a foley artist?

2   What genre of movies are known as "horse operas" in the movie business?

3   On a movie set, what job is done by the gaffer?

4   What was the name given to a plank of wood actors stood on to make them appear taller?

5   On a movie set what name is given to a microphone attached to a long pole?

6   Why does Ian Smithee sometimes appear at the end of movie credits?

7   What is arranged by a choreographer?

8   What is the name of the small truck that carries the camera and the camera operater?

9   What is the name of the board that is placed in front of camera before each shot?

10 What name is given to a cast member used to take the place of an actor for a specific scene?

ANSWERS

1. Sound effects 2. Westerns 3. Chief electrician 4. Pancake 5. Boom microphone 6. A director's alias 7. Dance sequence 8. Dolly 9. Clapperboard 10. Body double

QUIZ 204

• •

Which actor starred in

1 *One Fine Day, Dangerous Liaisons* and *Batman Returns*?

2 *Superman III, Harlem Nights* and *Stir Crazy*?

3 *Nine Months, The Lost World: Jurassic Park* and *Hannibal*?

4 *The Mexican, Twelve Monkeys* and *Meet Joe Black*?

5 *Breakfast at Tiffany's, My Fair Lady* and *Roman Holiday*?

6 *The Sound of Music, International Velvet* and *Waterloo*?

7 *Enemy of the State, The Legend of Bagger Vance* and *Independence Day*?

8 *Fletch, The Three Amigos* and *Spies Like Us*?

9 *The Defiant Ones, Guess Who's Coming to Dinner* and *To Sir with Love*?

10 *Overboard, The First Wives Club* and *Private Benjamin*?

ANSWERS

1. Michelle Pfeiffer 2. Richard Pryor 3. Julianne Moore 4. Brad Pitt 5. Audrey Hepburn 6. Christopher Plummer 7. Will Smith 8. Chevy Chase 9. Sidney Poitier 10. Goldie Hawn

QUIZ 205

• •

Who won these Oscars?

1　Best Actress – *As Good as it Gets*

2　Best Actor – *The Scent of a Woman*

3　Best Actor – *Kramer versus Kramer*

4　Best Actress – *The Accused*

5　Best Actor Oscar – *Amadeus*

6　Best Actress – *Annie Hall*

7　Best Actor – *To Kill a Mockingbird*

8　Best Actress – *The Piano*

9　Best Actress – *Driving Miss Daisy*

10　Best Actor – *Reversal of Fortune*

ANSWERS

1. Helen Hunt 2. Al Pacino 3. Dustin Hoffman 4. Jodie Foster 5. F Murray
Abraham 6. Diane Keaton 7. Gregory Peck 8. Holly Hunter 9. Jessica Tandy
10. Jeremy Irons

QUIZ 206

. . . .

1. What did the nuns change the title of "My Guy" to in *Sister Act*?

2. In which film did Michael Jackson sing 'Ease On Down The Road'?

3. Which song featured in the movies *Unchained* and *Ghost*?

4. The song "Big Spender" features in which movie and stage show?

5. Which character sang 'As Long as he Needs Me' in the musical *Oliver*?

6. Which Buddy Holly hit is also the title of a 1973 movie starring David Essex?

7. In which movie was Lee Marvin 'born under a wandrin' star'?

8. For which movie did Wet Wet Wet record the song 'Love is all Around'?

9. In which film did the Bill Haley rock and roll classic Rock Around The Clock first feature?

10. Who sang the Bond theme for *Tomorrow Never Dies*?

ANSWERS

1. "My God" 2. *The Wiz* 3. "Unchained Melody" 4. Sweet Charity 5. Nancy
6. "That'll be the Day" 7. *Paint Your Wagon* 8. *Four Weddings and a Funeral*
9. *The Blackboard Jungle* 10. Sheryl Crow

QUIZ 207

• •

1 What was The Beatles first movie?

2 What land did The Beatles venture into in the animated movie Yellow Submarine?

3 Which Beatles TV movie featured the songs, "The Fool On The Hill" and "I Am The Walrus"?

4 Which actor, famous for being Alf Garnett, played Abdul in Help?

5 Which movie starring Paul McCartney featured the song "No More Lonely Nights"?

6 What is the name of the movie production company established by George Harrison?

7 Are the Meanies in the movie Yellow Submarine, red, blue, yellow or green?

8 Which movie featuring The Beatles was also the name of one of their final studio album?

9 In which Monty Python movie did George Harrison play the cameo role of Mr Papadopolous?

10 Which 1967 black comedy set during World War II co-starred John Lennon?

ANSWERS

1. A Hard Day's Night 2. Pepperland 3. *The Magical Mystery Tour* 4. Warren Mitchell 5. Give my Regards to Broad Street 6. Handmade Films 7. Blue 8. Let it Be 9. The Life Of Brian 10. How I Won the War

QUIZ 208

• • • • • • • • • • • • • • • • • • •

1 Which movie features the characters Agent J and Agent K?

2 In which 2000 comedy did Jonathan Lipnicki play a young bloodsucker?

3 Which of the seven dwarfs wears glasses?

4 Which reptile is Indiana Jones terrified of?

5 What kind of animals are Scar and Simba?

6 Which Disney movie features the characters of Thomas O'Malley and Duchess?

7 In which movie do two dogs and a cat attempt to find their way home?

8 *The Adventure Home* and *The Rescue* are both sequels to which movie about a whale?

9 The song 'Walking in the Air' is heard in which animated movie?

10 In which movie did Cameron Diaz play the role of Mary?

ANSWERS

1. *Men in Black* 2. *The Little Vampire* 3. *Doc* 4. Snakes 5. Lions 6. *The Aristocats* 7. *Homeward Bound* 8. *Free Willy* 9. *The Snowman* 10. *There's Something About Mary*

QUIZ 209

1 The character of Milo Thatch appears in which Disney movie about a lost empire?

2 On what type of transport did E.T. and Elliot escape from government officials?

3 On whose novel was the film *National Velvet* based?

4 In which movie did King Louie sing 'I Wanna be like You'?

5 On screen what kind of animals are Skip, Benji and Rin Tin Tin?

6 In which direction does the cartoon mouse Fievel travel in a 1991 movie?

7 What is the name of the wood where Winnie the Pooh lives?

8 Which series of movies features the characters of Bilbo Baggins and Sauron?

9 Which 1999 teen comedy is also the title of a 2000 hit for Madonna?

10 In which war is *Pearl Harbor* set?

ANSWERS

1. *Atlantis* 2. Bicycles 3. Enid Bagnold 4. *The Jungle Book* 5. Dogs 6. West
7. Hundred Acre Wood 8. *The Lord of the Rings* 9. *American Pie* 10. World War II

QUIZ 210

• •

Unravel the anagrams to reveal the names of 10 movies.

1 GO NUN GUYS

2 GIST THEN

3 SCARE LOU

4 VINE FOR GUN

5 SHEENS HIS TEXT

6 I NIT CAT

7 BEN CLAM KIN

8 NAAN RIM

9 TON TAP

10 KEMON ROAR

ANSWERS

1. *Young Guns* 2. *The Sting* 3. *Carousel* 4. *Unforgiven* 5. *The Sixth Sense*
6. *Titanic* 7. *Men in Black* 8. *Rain Man* 9. *Patton* 10. *Moonraker*

QUIZ 211

Unravel the anagrams to reveal the names of 10 more movies.

1 HAD GIN

2 STUMP FORGER

3 BRED THIS

4 I LOVER

5 REV A BERTHA

6 CEDED POLO HUT

7 TOOL PAN

8 SUIT WHEY SEED

9 MUM BURN BED DAD

10 MEAN DRIPS

ANSWERS

1. *Gandhi* 2. *Forrest Gump* 3. *The Birds* 4. *Oliver* 5. *Braveheart* 6. *The Odd Couple* 7. *Platoon* 8. *Eyes Wide Shut* 9. *Dumb and Dumber* 10. *Spiderman*

QUIZ 212

• •

1 Who battled against aliens in Independence Day and against dinosaurs in *Jurassic Park*?

2 Which singer won an Oscar for her role in Moonstruck?

3 Which Australian pop star played the role of Lorna Campbell in the 2003 spy spoof, *Johnny English*?

4 Which movie tells the story of Jim Garrison's investigation into a 1963 assassination?

5 What was Marilyn Monroe's sweet first name in *Some Like It Hot*?

6 What was the first movie to feature the character of Indiana Jones?

7 Which hero has been played on film by many actors including Buster Crabbe, Christopher Lambert, Mike Henry and Lex Barker?

8 Which actor was born Archibald Leach?

9 In which 1991 movie does Billy Crystal embark on a cattle-driving holiday?

10 Which Kent born star of *The Lord Of The Rings* trilogy was voted Britain's Sexiest Actor in 2004?

ANSWERS

1. Jeff Goldblum 2. Cher 3. Natalie Imbruglia 4. JFK 5. Sugar 6. *Raiders of the Lost Ark* 7. Tarzan 8. Cary Grant 9. *City Slickers* 10. Orlando Bloom

QUIZ 213

• •

1   Who provided the voice of Mikey in *Look Who's Talking*?

2   Which actress played Honey Rider in *Dr. No*?

3   *Gone With The Wind* was set during which war?

4   In the 2003 action thriller *The League Of Extraordinary Gentlemen*, which author was portrayed by Shane West?

5   Which 2002 psychological thriller co-stars Al Pacino and Robin Williams?

6   Who played King Arthur in *Monty Python and the Holy Grail*?

7   What is the title of the sequel to *Bill and Ted's Excellent Adventure*?

8   The critically acclaimed 2002 film *Whale Rider* was set in which country?

9   In which comedy does Jim Carrey play a state trooper with a split personality?

10 Which infamous brothers were played by Gary and Martin Kemp in a 1990 movie?

ANSWERS

1. Bruce Willis 2. Ursula Andress 3. The American Civil War 4. Mark Twain
5. *Insomnia* 6. Graham Chapman 7. *Bill and Ted's Bogus Journey*
8. New Zealand 9. *Me, Myself and Irene* 10. *The Krays*

QUIZ 214

• •

Unravel the anagrams to reveal the names of 10 well-known movie characters

1 DOOR IN HOB

2 NAZ RAT

3 SEE MUCKY MOI

4 PERM HUT

5 DAN LAID

6 MI GLOW

7 PIN MOP SPRAY

8 NEW RING LADDY

9 COULD KAND

10 RED LACE NIL

ANSWERS

1. Robin Hood 2. Tarzan 3. Mickey Mouse 4. Thumper 5. Aladdin
6. Mowgli 7. Mary Poppins 8. Wendy Darling 9. Donald Duck
10. Cinderella

QUIZ 215

• •

Unravel the anagrams to reveal the names of 10 well-
known movie characters

1 MA BIB

2 PANT PEER

3 LACK DUD NOD

4 PACK IN A HOOT

5 HE NOT NGIKIL

6 FAB LUSH

7 SHE CRUEL

8 HERES HANK

9 I GLUES FAB

10 NICE N STORMS

ANSWERS

1. *Bambi* 2. Peter Pan 3. Donald Duck 4. *Captain Hook* 5. *The Lion King*
6. Bashful 7. Hercules 8. Shere Khan 9. *A Bug's Life* 10. *Monsters Inc.*

QUIZ 216

• •

1 Despite his tough guy image, what was John Wayne's real name?

2 Which 1968 movie, directed by and starring Wayne, was about the Vietnam War?

3 What word preceded Grande, Bravo and Lobo to give the titles of three John Wayne movies?

4 What was Joanne Dru wearing according to the title of a 1949 Wayne movie?

5 For which movie did he win his only Best Actor Oscar?

6 In which 1965 movie was Wayne reunited with his brothers at a funeral?

7 Which 1976 movie saw Wayne's last screen appearance as gunslinger J.B. Books?

8 Which ancient leader did he play in the 1953 movie The Conqueror?

9 In which 1952 movie, set in Ireland, did he co-star with Maureen O'Hara?

10 How did Wayne acquire his nickname, "The Duke"?

ANSWERS

1. Marion Morrison 2. *The Green Berets* 3. Rio 4. A yellow ribbon 5. *True Grit*
6. *The Sons of Katie Elder* 7. *The Shootist* 8. Genghis Khan 9. *The Quiet Man*
10. From his pet dog, Duke

QUIZ 217

• •

1   What is the first name of the character played by Kate Winslet in *Titanic*?

2   Who directed the 1997 movie *Titanic*?

3   In which ocean was the 1997 film *Titanic* set?

4   What was the title of Celine Dion's hit single from the movie *Titanic*?

5   In what year was the movie *Titanic* mostly set?

6   What is the first name of the character played by Leonardo DiCaprio?

7   Who played Cal Hockley, Kate Winslet's fiancée in the movie?

8   How many Oscar nominations did *Titanic* receive?

9   Which Oscar-winning actress played the role of Molly Brown?

10 Who plays Brock Lovett, the salvage operator, in the 1997 movie?

ANSWERS

1. Rose 2. James Cameron 3. Atlantic Ocean 4. 'My Heart Will Go On'
5. 1912 6. Jack 7. Billy Zane 8. 14 nominations, winning 11 9. Kathy Bates
10. Bill Paxton

QUIZ 218

. . . .

1 Which 1986 musical was a huge box-office flop for David Bowie and Patsy Kensit?

2 Whose adventures were a 1989 box-office flop for director Terry Gilliam?

3 Kevin Costner played the mariner in which expensive movie flop?

4 Which 1987 comedy flop set in Morocco starred Dustin Hoffman and Warren Beatty?

5 In which 1998 box-office flop was Harrison Ford marooned on a desert island?

6 Which 1995 movie panned by the critics saw Geena Davis playing a female pirate?

7 What was the name of the cat burglar played by Bruce Willis in the 1991 movie flop?

8 Which World War II movie starring John Belushi was a rare flop for Steven Spielberg?

9 Which 1980 western starring Kris Kristofferson was a financial disaster?

10 About which movie was it said, "It would have been cheaper to lower the Atlantic"?

ANSWERS

1. *Absolute Beginners* 2. Baron Munchausen 3. *Waterworld* 4. Ishtar 5. *Six Days and Seven Nights* 6. Cutthroat Island 7. Hudson Hawk 8. *1941* 9. *Heaven's Gate* 10. *Raise the Titanic*

QUIZ 219

• •

1 In which 1994 Star Trek movie did Captain Kirk join forces with Captain Picard?

2 Citizens were terminated at the age of 30 in which futuristic 1976 sci-fi movie?

3 What is the four-letter name of Marty McFly's foe in *Back to the Future*?

4 Which 1984 movie starring Sting is set in the year 10991 on the desert planet of Arakis?

5 To which planet did Arnold Schwarzenegger travel in *Total Recall*?

6 What make of car does Dr. Brown employ as a time machine in *Back to the Future*?

7 *The Road Warrior* and *Beyond Thunderdome* were sequels to which movie?

8 In which movie was an L.A. cop released from suspended animation in the year 2032?

9 James Caan is the star player of a violent sport of the future in which 1975 movie?

10 Kurt Russell attempts to rescue the U.S. president from a prison in which movie?

ANSWERS

1. *Star Trek: Generations* 2. *Logan's Run* 3. *Biff* 4. *Dune* 5. Mars 6. De Lorean
7. *Mad Max* 8. *Demolition Man* 9. *Rollerball* 10. *Escape from New York*

QUIZ 220

● ●

1 What is the name of the black- and red-faced villain in *Star Wars: The Phantom Menace*?

2 What plant is Count Dracula repelled by?

3 In which Christmas movie does Dudley Moore play an elf?

4 Which series of books by J.K. Rowling have been turned into blockbuster movies?

5 In a fairytale animated by Disney studios, who falls in love with Prince Charming?

6 Who played Ethan Hunt in the movie *Mission Impossible*?

7 Which movie star and rap artist played Muhammad Ali in the 2001 movie *Ali*?

8 Which actor links the roles of Indiana Jones, Han Solo and Dr. Kimble?

9 Which Disney animation is based on the novel Treasure Island?

10 What is Jim Carrey's occupation in the movie *Liar, Liar*?

ANSWERS

1. Darth Maul 2. Garlic 3. *Santa Claus: The Movie* 4. *Harry Potter* 5. Cinderella
6. Tom Cruise 7. Will Smith 8. Harrison Ford 9. *Treasure Planet* 10. Lawyer

QUIZ 221

1 What is the name of the Emperor who is the arch enemy of Buzz Lightyear?

2 Who recorded the song "I Don't Want to Miss a Thing" for *Armageddon*?

3 Who wrote the novel on which the musical *Oliver* was based?

4 Which star of the sitcom *Friends* appears in *Analyze This*?

5 Who plays the title role in the 2002 movie *Pluto Nash*?

6 Who does Robin Williams provide the voice for in Disney's *Aladdin*?

7 Which foe of Batman was played on screen by Jack Nicholson?

8 In which series of sci-fi thrillers does Sigourney Weaver play Ellen Ripley?

9 Which American pop sensation made her big screen debut in the movie *Crossroads*?

10 What sort of creature is Legolas in *The Lord of the Rings* trilogy?

ANSWERS

1. Emperor Zurg 2. Aerosmith 3. Charles Dickens 4. Lisa Kudrow 5. Eddie Murphy 6. The Genie 7. The Joker 8. *Alien* 9. Britney Spears 10. Elf

QUIZ 222

• •

1 What kind of animal is Pegasus in Disney's *Hercules*?

2 What kind of animal is Pummba in *The Lion King*?

3 What kind of animal is Andre in the movie of the same name?

4 What kind of birds were flying home in the movie *Fly Away Home*?

5 What kind of animal is Colonel Hathi in *The Jungle Book*?

6 What kind of animal is Wol in the Winnie the Pooh movies?

7 What kind of family pet is Cleo in *Pinocchio*?

8 What kind of animal is Orion in *Men in Black*?

9 What kind of animal is Sir Hiss in Disney's *Robin Hood*?

10 What kind of animal is Timothy in *Dumbo*?

ANSWERS

1. Horse 2. Warthog 3. Sea lion 4. Geese 5. Elephant 6. Owl 7. Goldfish
8. Cat 9. Snake 10. Mouse

QUIZ 255

• •

1 What kind of dinosaurs chased two children around the kitchen in *Jurassic Park*?

2 Which Disney movie featured a wicked witch called Maleficent?

3 What kind of insect attempts to be Pinocchio's conscience?

4 Which 2001 animated movie tells the story of a white blood cell cop called Ozzy?

5 In which movie do two dogs share a plate of spaghetti outside an Italian restaurant?

6 Which cartoon features a character called Chihiro whose parents are turned into pigs?

7 Which Disney movie set in the jungle is based on a novel by Edgar Rice Burroughs?

8 *Honey, I Blew Up the Kids* is the title of the sequel to which movie?

9 In which country are Bollywood movies made?

10 Which of the Muppets played Benjamina Gunn in *Muppet Treasure Island*?

QUIZ 256

• •

Fill in the missing place names in the following movie
  titles.

1 *The Purple Rose of…* starring Woody Allen

2 *Last Tango in…* starring Marlon Brando

3 *Funeral in…* starring Michael Caine

4 *Raising…* starring Nicholas Cage

5 *The Outlaw Josey…* starring Clint Eastwood

6 *Coming to…* starring Eddie Murphy

7 *Death on the…* starring Peter Ustinov

8 *The…House* starring Sean Connery

9 *The…Syndrome* starring Jane Fonda

10 *…Burning* starring Gene Hackman

ANSWERS

1. *Cairo* 2. *Paris* 3. *Berlin* 4. *Arizona* 5. *Wales* 6. *America* 7. *Nile* 8. *Russia*
9. *China* 10. *Mississippi*

QUIZ 257

. . . .

Fill in the missing animals in the following movie titles.

1 *The…in Winter* starring Peter O'Toole

2 *A Man called…* starring Richard Harris

3 *The Day of the…* starring Edward Fox

4 *…Day Afternoon* starring Al Pacino

5 *The Mighty…* starring Emilio Estevez

6 *Where…Dare s*tarring Richard Burton

7 *The Bad News…* starring Walter Matthau

8 *Kiss of the…Woman* starring William Hurt

9 *The Duchess and the Dirtwater…* starring George Segal

10 *…The Slayer* starring Jack Palance

ANSWERS

1. *Lion* 2. *Horse* 3. *Jackal* 4. *Dog* 5. *Ducks* 6. *Eagles* 7. *Bears* 8. *Spider* 9. *Fox*
10. *Hawk*

QUIZ 258

• •

1 Which coffin polisher went on to play the world's most secret agent?

2 Which star performed as a singer called Russ Le Roq in his early showbiz career?

3 As a teenager, which star played a character called Randy in the TV soap *Dallas*?

4 Which future star appeared with Brooke Shields in the movie *Endless Love*?

5 Which Oscar-winning star played Kip in the TV sitcom *Bosom Buddies*?

6 Which one of the Magnificent Seven played a wax dummy in *House of Wax*?

7 Which star danced with Bruce Springsteen in his 'Dancing in the Dark' video?

8 Which future comedy star had a small role in the Dirty Harry movie, *The Dead Pool*?

9 Who was on TV in Magnum PI and went on to star in movies such as *Casino*?

10 Which *Friends* star was Jim Carrey's leading lady in *Bruce Almighty*?

ANSWERS

1. Sean Connery 2. Russell Crowe 3. Brad Pitt 4. Tom Cruise 5. Tom Hanks
6. Charles Bronson 7. Courtney Cox 8. Jim Carrey 9. Sharon Stone
10. Jennifer Aniston

QUIZ 259

1 How many movies were made in the 20th century?

2 Who plays Rocky's brother-in-law Paulie in the movies?

3 Which pop group recorded the *Rocky* theme, 'Eye of the Tiger'?

4 Which star of The A-Team played the brutal boxer Clubber Lang in *Rocky III*?

5 Which U.S. city is the home city of Rocky?

6 In the *Rocky* movies, who plays his supportive girlfriend and wife, Adrian?

7 What is the name of the boxer played by Carl Weathers in the *Rocky* movies?

8 Who played the Russian boxer Ivan Drago in *Rocky IV*?

9 Who directed the 1976 movie *Rocky*?

10 What is Rocky's last name?

ANSWERS

1. Five 2. Burt Young 3. Survivor 4. Mr. T 5. Philadelphia 6. Talia Shire
7. Apollo Creed 8. Dolph Lungren 9. John G. Avildsen 10. Balboa

QUIZ 260

1 In which 1993 movie does Nicole Kidman play Michael Keaton's pregnant wife?

2 On which island was she born?

3 In which 1998 movie do Nicole and Sandra Bullock dabble in witchcraft?

4 Who directed Nicole in *Eyes Wide Shut*?

5 In which movie does she play a murderous TV reporter, Suzanne Maretto?

6 In which 2003 film did Nicole play the role of Ada Monroe?

7 In which 1988 thriller did she play Sam Neill's wife?

8 Nicole played Dr. Chase Meridian in which movie?

9 In which movie did she play Dustin Hoffman's moll?

10 In which year did Nicole marry Tom Cruise?

ANSWERS

1. *My Life* 2. Hawaii 3. *Practical Magic* 4. Stanley Kubrick 5. *To Die For*
6. *Cold Mountain* 7. *Dead Calm* 8. *Batman Forever* 9. *Billy Bathgate*
10. 1990

QUIZ 261

. . . .

1 What is the name of the character that Tom Cruise plays in the *Mission Impossible* movies?

2 In which 1992 movie did he cross-examine Jack Nicholson in a military courtroom?

3 Which movie sees Cruise mixing Pina Coladas and Harvey Wallbangers?

4 What was Cruise's pilot call sign in *Top Gun*?

5 In which movie, based on a John Grisham novel, did he play a Mafia lawyer?

6 Who was he married to from 1987 to 1990?

7 What was the occupation of the character played by Cruise in the film, *Eyes Wide Shut*?

8 Which 1988 film saw Tom Cruise mixing Pina Coladas?

9 Which movie earned him his first Oscar nomination?

10 Which sport featured in the movie *Days Of Thunder*?

ANSWERS

1. Ethan Hunt 2. *A Few Good Men* 3. *Cocktail* 4. *Maverick* 5. *The Firm*
6. Mimi Rogers 7. Doctor 8. *Cocktail* 9. *Born on the Fourth of July*
10. Stock car racing

QUIZ 262

• •

1 Who played Perry in Kevin & Perry Go Large?

2 Who wrote the novel upon which *Around The Wolrd In Eighty Days* is based?

3 What is the first name of Baron Frankenstein?

4 What connects Raising Cain and The Man in the Iron Mask?

5 In which 1985 comedy did Richard Pryor inherit millions of dollars?

6 In which movie with Nicholas Cage and John Travolta did Archer "borrow" Troy's face?

7 Which movie found David Tomlinson "on the bottom of the beautiful briny sea"?

8 Which of the Marx Brothers was born with the first name of Leonard?

9 In which 1995 movie did Michelle Pfeiffer become an inner-city schoolteacher?

10 The 1993 movie Dragon is a biopic of which martial arts hero?

ANSWERS

1. Kathy Burke 2. Jules Verne 3. Victor 4. The theme of twin brothers
5. Brewster's Millions 6. Face/Off 7. Bedknobs and Broomsticks 8. Chico
9. Dangerous Minds 10. Bruce Lee

QUIZ 263

• •

1 Who connects the epics Lawrence of Arabia, Ulysses and Barabbas?

2 Who has been played on screen by Bo Derek, Dorothy Dunbar and Maureen O'Sullivan?

3 Who played the President of the U.S.A. in Primary Colors?

4 How are Curly, Larry and Mo collectively known?

5 Who played Oscar Madison in The Odd Couple?

6 What game is played by Steve McQueen and Faye Dunaway in The Thomas Crown Affair?

7 Who was the first British star to win a Best Actress Oscar?

8 Who played Henry VIII in Carry On Henry?

9 Which writer did Virginia McKenna portray in Born Free?

10 In Peter's Friends which British comedy star played Peter?

ANSWERS

1. Anthony Quinn 2. Tarzan's Jane 3. John Travolta 4. The Three Stooges
5. Walter Matthau 6. Chess 7. Vivien Leigh 8. Sid James 9. Joy Adamson
10. Stephen Fry

QUIZ 264

1 Which martial arts expert stars alongside Steve Coogan in the 2004 film *Around The World In Eighty Days*?

2 Who played Dr. Strangelove in the 1964 movie?

3 In which 1986 picture did Judge Reinhold and Helen Slater kidnap Bette Midler?

4 In Alfred Hitchcock's *The Trouble with Harry*, what was Harry's trouble?

5 Which 1996 movie set in Scotland features the characters of Spud, Renton and Begbie?

6 During which war was *Catch 22* set?

7 Who played the role of Martin Weir in the black comedy *Get Shorty*?

8 Upon which ancient novel was the film *Oh Brother, Where Art Thou?* based?

9 Who played Hannah in the Woody Allen comedy *Hannah and Her Sisters*?

10 In which movie classic did Alec Guinness play eight members of the d'Ascoyne family?

ANSWERS

1. Jackie Chan 2. Peter Sellers 3. *Ruthless People* 4. A corpse
5. *Trainspotting* 6. World War II 7. Danny DeVito 8. *The Odyssey* 9. Mia
Farrow 10. *Kind Hearts and Coronets*

QUIZ 265

• •

1   Which German screen icon played the leading lady in *The Blue Angel*?

2   Who directed *Crouching Tiger, Hidden Dragon*?

3   In which capital city is Frederico Fellini's La Dolce Vita set?

4   Which 1922 horror classic sees Max Schreck playing a vampire?

5   On which Shakespeare play was the Japanese movie *Ran* based?

6   *The Magnificent Seven* was based on which classic foreign movie?

7   In which 1956 movie did Max von Sydow play a knight returning from the Crusades?

8   Which French actor played the title role in Monsieur Hulot's Holiday?

9   Which French pin-up connects *Viva Maria*, *Vie Privée* and *Helen of Troy*?

10 Who played the title role in the 2001 Oscar nominated movie *Amelie*?

ANSWERS

1. Marlene Dietrich 2. Ang Lee 3. Rome 4. Nosferatu 5. King Lear 6. The Seven Samurai 7. The Seventh Seal 8. Jacques Tati 9. Brigitte Bardot 10. Audrey Tautou

QUIZ 266

• •

1   On whose novel was the 1968 horror *The Devil Rides Out* based?

2   Which movie based on George Orwell's novel was Richard Burton's final role?

3   In which adaptation of a Dickens' novel did Jean Cadell play Mrs. Micawber?

4   Which war movie co-starring Lee Marvin, was based on a novel by E.M. Nathanson?

5   Who wrote the novels from which *Watership Down* and *The Plague Dogs* were adapted?

6   Who played Fagin in the 1968 movie version of Charles Dickens' novel *Oliver Twist*?

7   Which F. Scott Fitzgerald novel was remade in 1974 starring Robert Redford?

8   Whose novel *A Clockwork Orange* was adapted into a controversial movie?

9   What is the title of the novel on which the Oscar-winning movie *Schindler's List* is based?

10 Which Robert Louis Stevenson novel, filmed in 1960, features a hero called David Balfour?

ANSWERS

1. Dennis Wheatley 2. 1984 3. David Copperfield 4. The Dirty Dozen
5. Richard Adams 6. Ron Moody 7. The Great Gatsby 8. Anthony Burgess
9. Schindler's Ark 10. Kidnapped

QUIZ 267

1 In which 1965 picture did Jack Lemmon play the evil Professor Fate?

2 In which 1978 movie did Kris Kristofferson use the call sign Rubber Duck?

3 Which 1991 road movie saw Michael Madsen play Susan Sarandon's boyfriend?

4 Who played Smokey in the 1977 movie *Smokey and the Bandit*?

5 Which 1981 comedy tells the story of a road race from Connecticut to California?

6 What was the last road movie made by Bob Hope and Bing Crosby, filmed in 1962?

7 Which movie featured Whoopi Goldberg and Drew Barrymore driving across the U.S.A.?

8 In which 1954 picture did Marlon Brando play the leader of a motorcycle gang?

9 Chevy Chase, John Belushi and Emilio Estevez have each starred in which series of movies?

10 Who played Captain America in *Easy Rider*?

ANSWERS

1. *The Great Race* 2. *Convoy* 3. *Thelma and Louise* 4. Jackie Gleason 5. *The Cannonball Run* 6. *Road to Hong Kong* 7. *Boys on the Side* 8. *The Wild One* 9. *National Lampoon's* 10. Peter Fonda

QUIZ 268

• •

What was the name of...

1 The car in The Love Bug?

2 The prospector in *Toy Story II*?

3 The baby son of Barney Rubble?

4 The evil uncle in *The Lion King*?

5 The fairy in *Peter Pan*?

6 The one-legged pirate in *Treasure Island*?

7 The female mouse in *The Rescuers*?

8 The pet dog of *The Grinch*?

9 The town ruled by Lord Farquaad in *Shrek*?

10 The Emperor in *The Emperor's New Groove*

ANSWERS

1. Herbie 2. Stinky Pete 3. Bam Bam 4. Scar 5. Tinkerbell 6. Long John
Silver 7. Bianca 8. Max 9. Duloc 10. Kuzco

QUIZ 269

. . . .

What was the name of...

1 Popeye's archenemy?

2 The gang of children in Never Never Land?

3 The droid played by Kenny Baker in *Star Wars*?

4 Dumbo the elephant's mother?

5 The eldest son of Gomez and Morticia Addams?

6 The panther in *The Jungle Book*?

7 The group of miners who sang, "Heigh Ho"?

8 The character played by Linda Cardellini in *Scooby Doo*?

9 Juni's sister in *Spy Kids*?

10 The magical flying white horse in *Hercules*?

ANSWERS

1. Bluto 2. The Lost Boys 3. R2-D2 4. Mrs. Jumbo 5. Pugsley 6. Bagheera
7. Seven Dwarfs 8. Velma 9. Carmen 10. Pegasus

QUIZ 270

1 In which movie did Kirk Douglas play a Norse warrior called Einar?

2 Which 1959 epic saw Charlton Heston competing in a chariot race?

3 Cecil B. de Mille made two versions of which biblical epic?

4 Which goddess did Honor Blackman play in *Jason and the Argonauts*?

5 Who played Samson in the 1950 epic *Samson and Delilah*?

6 Which 1960 movie tells the story of a Roman slave who led a slave's revolt?

7 Which Emperor was played by Peter Ustinov in *Quo Vadis*?

8 Which epic of the 1930s was billed as, "Margaret Mitchell's story of the Old South"?

9 On whose novel was the 1984 movie *A Passage to India* based?

10 Who plays Count Almasy in the 1996 Oscar-winning *The English Patient*?

ANSWERS

1. The Vikings 2. *Ben Hur* 3. *The Ten Commandments* 4. Hera 5. Victor Mature 6. *Spartacus* 7. The Emperor Nero 8. *Gone With The Wind* 9. E.M. Forster 10. Ralph Fiennes

QUIZ 255

• •

1 What kind of dinosaurs chased two children around the kitchen in *Jurassic Park*?

2 Which Disney movie featured a wicked witch called Maleficent?

3 What kind of insect attempts to be Pinocchio's conscience?

4 Which 2001 animated movie tells the story of a white blood cell cop called Ozzy?

5 In which movie do two dogs share a plate of spaghetti outside an Italian restaurant?

6 Which cartoon features a character called Chihiro whose parents are turned into pigs?

7 Which Disney movie set in the jungle is based on a novel by Edgar Rice Burroughs?

8 *Honey, I Blew Up the Kids* is the title of the sequel to which movie?

9 In which country are Bollywood movies made?

10 Which of the Muppets played Benjamina Gunn in *Muppet Treasure Island*?

ANSWERS

1. Velociraptors 2. *Sleeping Beauty* 3. A cricket called Jiminy Cricket
4. Osmosis Jones 5. *Lady and the Tramp* 6. *Spirited Away* 7. Tarzan
8. *Honey, I Shrunk the Kids* 9. India 10. Miss Piggy

QUIZ 256

• •

Fill in the missing place names in the following movie
   titles.

1   *The Purple Rose of…* starring Woody Allen
2   *Last Tango in…* starring Marlon Brando
3   *Funeral in…* starring Michael Caine
4   *Raising…* starring Nicholas Cage
5   *The Outlaw Josey…* starring Clint Eastwood
6   *Coming to…* starring Eddie Murphy
7   *Death on the…* starring Peter Ustinov
8   *The…House* starring Sean Connery
9   *The…Syndrome* starring Jane Fonda
10 *…Burning* starring Gene Hackman

ANSWERS

1. *Cairo* 2. *Paris* 3. *Berlin* 4. *Arizona* 5. *Wales* 6. *America* 7. *Nile* 8. *Russia*
9. *China* 10. *Mississippi*

QUIZ 257

• •

Fill in the missing animals in the following movie titles.

1 *The…in Winter* starring Peter O'Toole

2 *A Man called…* starring Richard Harris

3 *The Day of the…* starring Edward Fox

4 *…Day Afternoon* starring Al Pacino

5 *The Mighty…* starring Emilio Estevez

6 *Where…Dare* starring Richard Burton

7 *The Bad News…* starring Walter Matthau

8 *Kiss of the…Woman* starring William Hurt

9 *The Duchess and the Dirtwater…* starring George Segal

10 *…The Slayer* starring Jack Palance

ANSWERS

1. *Lion* 2. *Horse* 3. *Jackal* 4. *Dog* 5. *Ducks* 6. *Eagles* 7. *Bears* 8. *Spider* 9. *Fox* 10. *Hawk*

QUIZ 258

• •

1 Which coffin polisher went on to play the world's most secret agent?

2 Which star performed as a singer called Russ Le Roq in his early showbiz career?

3 As a teenager, which star played a character called Randy in the TV soap *Dallas*?

4 Which future star appeared with Brooke Shields in the movie *Endless Love*?

5 Which Oscar-winning star played Kip in the TV sitcom *Bosom Buddies*?

6 Which one of the Magnificent Seven played a wax dummy in *House of Wax*?

7 Which star danced with Bruce Springsteen in his 'Dancing in the Dark' video?

8 Which future comedy star had a small role in the Dirty Harry movie, *The Dead Pool*?

9 Who was on TV in Magnum PI and went on to star in movies such as *Casino*?

10 Which *Friends* star was Jim Carrey's leading lady in *Bruce Almighty*?

ANSWERS

1. Sean Connery 2. Russell Crowe 3. Brad Pitt 4. Tom Cruise 5. Tom Hanks
6. Charles Bronson 7. Courtney Cox 8. Jim Carrey 9. Sharon Stone
10. Jennifer Aniston

QUIZ 259

. . . .

1 How many movies were made in the 20th century?

2 Who plays Rocky's brother-in-law Paulie in the movies?

3 Which pop group recorded the *Rocky* theme, 'Eye of the Tiger'?

4 Which star of The A-Team played the brutal boxer Clubber Lang in *Rocky III*?

5 Which U.S. city is the home city of Rocky?

6 In the *Rocky* movies, who plays his supportive girlfriend and wife, Adrian?

7 What is the name of the boxer played by Carl Weathers in the *Rocky* movies?

8 Who played the Russian boxer Ivan Drago in *Rocky IV*?

9 Who directed the 1976 movie *Rocky*?

10 What is Rocky's last name?

ANSWERS

1. Five 2. Burt Young 3. Survivor 4. Mr. T 5. Philadelphia 6. Talia Shire
7. Apollo Creed 8. Dolph Lungren 9. John G. Avildsen 10. Balboa

QUIZ 260

. . . .

1 In which 1993 movie does Nicole Kidman play Michael Keaton's pregnant wife?

2 On which island was she born?

3 In which 1998 movie do Nicole and Sandra Bullock dabble in witchcraft?

4 Who directed Nicole in *Eyes Wide Shut*?

5 In which movie does she play a murderous TV reporter, Suzanne Maretto?

6 In which 2003 film did Nicole play the role of Ada Monroe?

7 In which 1988 thriller did she play Sam Neill's wife?

8 Nicole played Dr. Chase Meridian in which movie?

9 In which movie did she play Dustin Hoffman's moll?

10 In which year did Nicole marry Tom Cruise?

ANSWERS

1. *My Life* 2. Hawaii 3. *Practical Magic* 4. Stanley Kubrick 5. *To Die For*
6. *Cold Mountain* 7. *Dead Calm* 8. *Batman Forever* 9. *Billy Bathgate*
10. 1990

QUIZ 261

• •

1 What is the name of the character that Tom Cruise plays in the *Mission Impossible* movies?

2 In which 1992 movie did he cross-examine Jack Nicholson in a military courtroom?

3 Which movie sees Cruise mixing Pina Coladas and Harvey Wallbangers?

4 What was Cruise's pilot call sign in *Top Gun*?

5 In which movie, based on a John Grisham novel, did he play a Mafia lawyer?

6 Who was he married to from 1987 to 1990?

7 What was the occupation of the character played by Cruise in the film, *Eyes Wide Shut*?

8 Which 1988 film saw Tom Cruise mixing Pina Coladas?

9 Which movie earned him his first Oscar nomination?

10 Which sport featured in the movie *Days Of Thunder*?

ANSWERS

1. Ethan Hunt 2. *A Few Good Men* 3. *Cocktail* 4. *Maverick* 5. *The Firm*
6. Mimi Rogers 7. Doctor 8. *Cocktail* 9. *Born on the Fourth of July*
10. Stock car racing

QUIZ 262

• •

1   Who played Perry in Kevin & Perry Go Large?

2   Who wrote the novel upon which *Around The Wolrd In Eighty Days* is based?

3   What is the first name of Baron Frankenstein?

4   What connects Raising Cain and The Man in the Iron Mask?

5   In which 1985 comedy did Richard Pryor inherit millions of dollars?

6   In which movie with Nicholas Cage and John Travolta did Archer "borrow" Troy's face?

7   Which movie found David Tomlinson "on the bottom of the beautiful briny sea"?

8   Which of the Marx Brothers was born with the first name of Leonard?

9   In which 1995 movie did Michelle Pfeiffer become an inner-city schoolteacher?

10 The 1993 movie Dragon is a biopic of which martial arts hero?

ANSWERS

1. Kathy Burke   2. Jules Verne   3. Victor   4. The theme of twin brothers
5. Brewster's Millions   6. Face/Off   7. Bedknobs and Broomsticks   8. Chico
9. Dangerous Minds   10. Bruce Lee

QUIZ 263

. . . .

1 Who connects the epics Lawrence of Arabia, Ulysses and Barabbas?

2 Who has been played on screen by Bo Derek, Dorothy Dunbar and Maureen O'Sullivan?

3 Who played the President of the U.S.A. in Primary Colors?

4 How are Curly, Larry and Mo collectively known?

5 Who played Oscar Madison in The Odd Couple?

6 What game is played by Steve McQueen and Faye Dunaway in The Thomas Crown Affair?

7 Who was the first British star to win a Best Actress Oscar?

8 Who played Henry VIII in Carry On Henry?

9 Which writer did Virginia McKenna portray in Born Free?

10 In Peter's Friends which British comedy star played Peter?

ANSWERS

1. Anthony Quinn 2. Tarzan's Jane 3. John Travolta 4. The Three Stooges
5. Walter Matthau 6. Chess 7. Vivien Leigh 8. Sid James 9. Joy Adamson
10. Stephen Fry

QUIZ 264

• •

1 Which martial arts expert stars alongside Steve Coogan in the 2004 film *Around The World In Eighty Days*?

2 Who played Dr. Strangelove in the 1964 movie?

3 In which 1986 picture did Judge Reinhold and Helen Slater kidnap Bette Midler?

4 In Alfred Hitchcock's *The Trouble with Harry*, what was Harry's trouble?

5 Which 1996 movie set in Scotland features the characters of Spud, Renton and Begbie?

6 During which war was *Catch 22* set?

7 Who played the role of Martin Weir in the black comedy *Get Shorty*?

8 Upon which ancient novel was the film *Oh Brother, Where Art Thou?* based?

9 Who played Hannah in the Woody Allen comedy *Hannah and Her Sisters*?

10 In which movie classic did Alec Guinness play eight members of the d'Ascoyne family?

ANSWERS

1. Jackie Chan 2. Peter Sellers 3. *Ruthless People* 4. A corpse
5. *Trainspotting* 6. World War II 7. Danny DeVito 8. *The Odyssey* 9. Mia
Farrow 10. *Kind Hearts and Coronets*

QUIZ 265

1   Which German screen icon played the leading lady in *The Blue Angel*?

2   Who directed *Crouching Tiger, Hidden Dragon*?

3   In which capital city is Frederico Fellini's La Dolce Vita set?

4   Which 1922 horror classic sees Max Schreck playing a vampire?

5   On which Shakespeare play was the Japanese movie *Ran* based?

6   *The Magnificent Seven* was based on which classic foreign movie?

7   In which 1956 movie did Max von Sydow play a knight returning from the Crusades?

8   Which French actor played the title role in Monsieur Hulot's Holiday?

9   Which French pin-up connects *Viva Maria*, *Vie Privée* and *Helen of Troy*?

10 Who played the title role in the 2001 Oscar nominated movie *Amelie*?

ANSWERS

1. Marlene Dietrich 2. Ang Lee 3. Rome 4. Nosferatu 5. King Lear 6. The Seven Samurai 7. The Seventh Seal 8. Jacques Tati 9. Brigitte Bardot 10. Audrey Tautou

QUIZ 266

. . . .

1 On whose novel was the 1968 horror *The Devil Rides Out* based?

2 Which movie based on George Orwell's novel was Richard Burton's final role?

3 In which adaptation of a Dickens' novel did Jean Cadell play Mrs. Micawber?

4 Which war movie co-starring Lee Marvin, was based on a novel by E.M. Nathanson?

5 Who wrote the novels from which *Watership Down* and *The Plague Dogs* were adapted?

6 Who played Fagin in the 1968 movie version of Charles Dickens' novel *Oliver Twist*?

7 Which F. Scott Fitzgerald novel was remade in 1974 starring Robert Redford?

8 Whose novel *A Clockwork Orange* was adapted into a controversial movie?

9 What is the title of the novel on which the Oscar-winning movie *Schindler's List* is based?

10 Which Robert Louis Stevenson novel, filmed in 1960, features a hero called David Balfour?

ANSWERS

1. Dennis Wheatley 2. 1984 3. David Copperfield 4. The Dirty Dozen
5. Richard Adams 6. Ron Moody 7. The Great Gatsby 8. Anthony Burgess
9. Schindler's Ark 10. Kidnapped

QUIZ 267

• •

1 In which 1965 picture did Jack Lemmon play the evil Professor Fate?

2 In which 1978 movie did Kris Kristofferson use the call sign Rubber Duck?

3 Which 1991 road movie saw Michael Madsen play Susan Sarandon's boyfriend?

4 Who played Smokey in the 1977 movie *Smokey and the Bandit*?

5 Which 1981 comedy tells the story of a road race from Connecticut to California?

6 What was the last road movie made by Bob Hope and Bing Crosby, filmed in 1962?

7 Which movie featured Whoopi Goldberg and Drew Barrymore driving across the U.S.A.?

8 In which 1954 picture did Marlon Brando play the leader of a motorcycle gang?

9 Chevy Chase, John Belushi and Emilio Estevez have each starred in which series of movies?

10 Who played Captain America in *Easy Rider*?

ANSWERS

1. *The Great Race* 2. *Convoy* 3. *Thelma and Louise* 4. Jackie Gleason 5. *The Cannonball Run* 6. *Road to Hong Kong* 7. *Boys on the Side* 8. *The Wild One* 9. *National Lampoon's* 10. Peter Fonda

QUIZ 268

. . . .

What was the name of...

1 The car in The Love Bug?

2 The prospector in *Toy Story II*?

3 The baby son of Barney Rubble?

4 The evil uncle in *The Lion King*?

5 The fairy in *Peter Pan*?

6 The one-legged pirate in *Treasure Island*?

7 The female mouse in *The Rescuers*?

8 The pet dog of *The Grinch*?

9 The town ruled by Lord Farquaad in *Shrek*?

10 The Emperor in *The Emperor's New Groove*

ANSWERS

1. Herbie 2. Stinky Pete 3. Bam Bam 4. Scar 5. Tinkerbell 6. Long John
Silver 7. Bianca 8. Max 9. Duloc 10. Kuzco

QUIZ 269

• •

What was the name of...

1 Popeye's archenemy?

2 The gang of children in Never Never Land?

3 The droid played by Kenny Baker in *Star Wars*?

4 Dumbo the elephant's mother?

5 The eldest son of Gomez and Morticia Addams?

6 The panther in *The Jungle Book*?

7 The group of miners who sang, "Heigh Ho"?

8 The character played by Linda Cardellini in *Scooby Doo*?

9 Juni's sister in *Spy Kids*?

10 The magical flying white horse in *Hercules*?

ANSWERS

1. Bluto 2. The Lost Boys 3. R2-D2 4. Mrs. Jumbo 5. Pugsley 6. Bagheera
7. Seven Dwarfs 8. Velma 9. Carmen 10. Pegasus

QUIZ 270

. . . .

1 In which movie did Kirk Douglas play a Norse warrior called Einar?

2 Which 1959 epic saw Charlton Heston competing in a chariot race?

3 Cecil B. de Mille made two versions of which biblical epic?

4 Which goddess did Honor Blackman play in *Jason and the Argonauts*?

5 Who played Samson in the 1950 epic *Samson and Delilah*?

6 Which 1960 movie tells the story of a Roman slave who led a slave's revolt?

7 Which Emperor was played by Peter Ustinov in *Quo Vadis*?

8 Which epic of the 1930s was billed as, "Margaret Mitchell's story of the Old South"?

9 On whose novel was the 1984 movie *A Passage to India* based?

10 Who plays Count Almasy in the 1996 Oscar-winning *The English Patient*?

ANSWERS

1. The Vikings 2. *Ben Hur* 3. *The Ten Commandments* 4. Hera 5. Victor Mature 6. *Spartacus* 7. The Emperor Nero 8. *Gone With The Wind* 9. E.M. Forster 10. Ralph Fiennes

QUIZ 271

• •

1 Which studio made the Carry On movies?

2 What is the name of the lion that appears in the opening credits of all MGM movies?

3 A mountain peak surrounded by stars is the logo of which studio?

4 Why was the sorcerer called Yensid in the animated movie *Fantasia*?

5 "The Proud Lady" is the nickname given to which movie studio's logo?

6 Which London studios made The Lavender Hill Mob and The Blue Lamp?

7 Four siblings called Albert, Harry, Jack and Sam founded which studio?

8 The British company Hammer Films is known for making which genre of movies?

9 Which company founded in 1912 announced a $65 million loss in 1998?

10 Which studio made the animated movie *Chicken Run*?

ANSWERS

1. Pinewood Studios 2. Leo 3. Paramount 4. Yensid is Disney spelt backwards 5. Columbia 6. Ealing Studios 7. Warner Brothers 8. Horror movies 9. Universal Studios 10. DreamWorks

QUIZ 272

. . . .

1   What is the name of Dorothy's dog in The Wizard of Oz?

2   Which U.S. state is home to Dorothy?

3   In the movie what is the name of the cowardly lion?

4   Which race of small people advised Dorothy to "follow the yellow brick road"?

5   Which character was portrayed by Ray Bolger?

6   What is the name of Dorothy's aunt in The Wizard of Oz?

7   What does Dorothy say three times when she taps the heels of her ruby slippers together?

8   On whose novel is the movie based?

9   Name the actor who played the Wizard of Oz.

10 To which city does Dorothy travel to meet the "wonderful Wizard of Oz"?

ANSWERS

1. Toto 2. Kansas 3. Zeke 4. Munchkins 5. The Scarecrow 6. Auntie Em
7. "There's no place like home" 8. L. Frank Baum 9. Frank Morgan 10. The Emerald City

QUIZ 273

• •

1 In The Great Escape who attempted to escape from his pursuers on a motorcycle?

2 Name the actor who played the "Tunnel King" and suffered from claustrophobia.

3 Which actor was shot in the back on a railway line whilst attempting to escape?

4 What code name was given to the character played by Richard Attenborough?

5 In The Great Escape, who played "The Forger"?

6 What was the nationality of the character played by James Coburn in the movie?

7 Which Scottish actor played the intelligence officer at the P.O.W. camp?

8 Which singer, who topped the 60s charts with the song, "Johnny Remember Me", played the role of William "The Tunneller" Dickes in The Great Escape?

9 Who played the "Scrounger" in the movie?

10 Who directed The Great Escape?

ANSWERS

1. Steve McQueen 2. Charles Bronson 3. David McCallum 4. Big X
5. Donald Pleasance 6. Australian 7. Gordon Jackson 8. John Leyton
9. James Garner 10. John Sturges

QUIZ 274

. . . .

1　Which star of the TV series *The Young Ones*, played Fred in *Drop Dead Fred*?

2　In which 1997 thriller did Brad Pitt play a terrorist called Frankie Maguire?

3　What is the title of the fourth movie to feature the character of Hannibal Lecter?

4　For which comedy did a choir mistress called Iris Stevenson provide the inspiration?

5　Who played Sergeant Emil Foley in *An Officer and a Gentleman*?

6　In *E.T.*, a spacecraft abandons E.T. in the suburbs of which U.S. city?

7　In which 1985 thriller did Glenn Close defend Jeff Bridges against a murder charge?

8　In the movie *Three Men and a Baby*, who played the character called Pete Mitchell?

9　Which of the Marx Brothers shares his name with Oprah Winfrey's production company?

10　Who died in *The Towering Inferno* and went on to star in the TV series *Hart to Hart*?

ANSWERS

1. Rik Mayall 2. *The Devil's Own* 3. Red Dragon 4. *Sister Act* 5. Louis Gossett Jr. 6. Los Angeles 7. Jagged Edge 8. Tom Selleck 9. Harpo
10. Robert Wagner

QUIZ 275

• •

1   In which musical did Clint Eastwood co-star with Jean Seberg?

2   In which movie did Jack Nicholson share a bedroom scene with Michelle Pfeiffer?

3   Name the political activist killed in 1922 and played on screen by Liam Neeson.

4   Which country holds a festival that awards *The Golden Bear* to the best movie?

5   On screen Robert Redford and Paul Newman carried out 'The Sting' in which city?

6   In which 1999 picture does Sean Connery attempt to steal a priceless Chinese mask?

7   What is the surname of the owners of the chicken farm in *Chicken Run*?

8   Which Spielburg produced TV mini-series told the story of the Keys, the Crawfords and the Clarkes and their involvement in alien abductions?

9   In which musical did Richard Harris portray King Arthur?

10 In which century was the epic *El Cid* set?

ANSWERS

1. *Paint Your Wagon*   2. *The Witches of Eastwick*   3. Michael Collins
4. Germany   5. Chicago   6. *Entrapment*   7. Tweedy   8. *Taken*   9. *Camelot*
10. 11th century

QUIZ 276

1 From which London train station does the Hogwart's Express depart?

2 Who plays Harry Potter?

3 Which actor played Albus Dumbedore in the first two movies?

4 What was *Harry Potter and the Philosopher's Stone* called in the U.S.?

5 What is the name of Harry Potter's uncle, played on screen by Richard Griffiths?

6 In the Harry Potter movies, who is portrayed by Rupert Grint?

7 Who plays the character of Gilderoy Lockhart in the second Harry Potter movie?

8 What is the name of the professor played by Alan Rickman?

9 What is Hagrid's three-headed dog called?

10 Is the Hogwart's Express black, red or green?

ANSWERS

QUIZ 277

• •

1 What breed of dog is the Colonel in the 101 Dalmations animated movie?

2 In the cartoon movie what is the name of the Dalmatian puppy that is forever hungry?

3 Who does Glenn Close portray in the live-action version of the story?

4 In the Disney animation what is the name of the dog who fathers the Dalmatians?

5 What is the name of the cat who helps the Dalmatians escape from their kidnappers?

6 What did Princess and Duchess give to the Dalmatians on their travels?

7 What type of bird is Lucy in the cartoon version?

8 How does Roger earn his living in 101 Dalmatians?

9 In the Disney cartoon, what is the name of Roger's wife?

10 Who wrote the novel on which the movies are based?

ANSWERS

1. Old English Sheepdog 2. Roly 3. Cruella DeVil 4. Pongo 5. Sergeant Tibbs 6. Milk, as they are both cows 7. Goose 8. Songwriter 9. Anita 10. Penned by Dodie Smith

QUIZ 278

1. Which 2001 comedy included appearances by Jeffrey Archer and Salman Rushdie?

2. Which Nazi was portrayed by Gregory Peck in The Boys from Brazil?

3. In which movie did Nick Nolte fall in love with Barbra Streisand?

4. Who was the only English-born actor to win a Best Actor Oscar in the 1990s?

5. When Alec Guinness portrayed Fagin who played Bill Sikes?

6. When Errol Flynn played Robin Hood who did Alan Hale portray?

7. Which war movie told the story of the German counter-attack in the Ardennes?

8. In a Disney movie whose voices were provided by Paige O'Hara and Robby Benson?

9. In 1932, which European city hosted the world's first movie festival?

10. Who played Tarzan when Bo Derek played Jane?

ANSWERS

1. *Bridget Jones's Diary* 2. Josef Mengele 3. *The Prince of Tides* 4. Jeremy Irons 5. Robert Newton 6. Little John 7. *The Battle of the Bulge* 8. *Beauty and the Beast* 9. Venice 10. Miles O'Keefe

QUIZ 279

. . . .

1 What was the first X-rated movie to win the Best Picture Oscar?

2 What was the name of the newspaper that Kane owned and ran in Citizen Kane?

3 Which movie star became the first stepmother to Carrie Fisher?

4 Which 1987 movie starring Oliver Reed was based on Lucy Irving's autobiography?

5 Which pop star replaced Michael Caine as Alfie in the 1975 sequel *Alfie Darling*?

6 What part was played by both Cary Grant and Michael Hordern in *Alice in Wonderland*?

7 Who narrated the 1993 western *Tombstone*, starring Kurt Russell as Wyatt Earp?

8 The 1996 movie *The Birdcage* was a remake of which French movie?

9 In which U.S. state was *The Blair Witch Project* set?

10 In which century was the sci-fi fantasy *Barbarella* set?

ANSWERS

1. *Midnight Cowboy* 2. *The Inquirer* 3. Elizabeth Taylor 4. *Castaway* 5. Alan Price 6. Mock Turtle 7. Robert Mitchum 8. La Cage aux Folles 9. Maryland 10. 40th century

QUIZ 280

• •

1 Which 1984 fantasy saw the character of Bastian entering the land of *Fantasia*?

2 In which 1982 movie did John Cleese play Robin Hood and Ian Holm play Napoleon?

3 What was the title of the movie in which David Bowie played the evil Goblin King?

4 Which movie tells the story of an orphan raised by a group called the Mystics?

5 In which 1988 movie did Val Kilmer play a swashbuckling warrior called Madmartigan?

6 Laurence Olivier played the Greek God Zeus in which 1981 classic?

7 Who played opposite Cyd Charisse in the 1954 musical *Brigadoon*?

8 Nigel Terry played King Arthur in which 1981 movie?

9 Which 1987 fantasy featured cameo appearances by Peter Falk and Billy Crystal?

10 Who played the role of a young Wendy Darling in the Spielberg movie *Hook*?

ANSWERS

1. *The Never Ending Story* 2. *Time Bandits* 3. *Labyrinth* 4. *The Dark Crystal*
5. *Willow* 6. *Clash of the Titans* 7. Gene Kelly 8. *Excalibur* 9. *The Princess Bride*
10. Gwyneth Paltrow

QUIZ 281

• •

1. Robert Redford and Barbra Streisand played lovers in which 1973 picture?

2. In which 1991 movie did Al Pacino play a cook who woos waitress Michelle Pfeiffer?

3. In the Cary Grant romantic comedy *Bringing up Baby*, what kind of wild cat is Baby?

4. In which 1984 movie did Tom Hanks fall in love with a mermaid?

5. Who romanced Humphrey Bogart in *To Have and Have Not* and then married him?

6. Which movie star died in 1926 after appearing in *The Sheik and the Eagle*?

7. In which 1987 picture did Nicholas Cage confess, "I'm in love with you" to Cher?

8. Where did Celia Johnson and Trevor Howard conduct a love affair in *Brief Encounter*?

9. Who played Shakespeare in the 1998 movie *Shakespeare in Love*?

10. Who played the bride in the 1997 romantic comedy *My Best Friend's Wedding*?

ANSWERS

1. *The Way We Were* 2. *Frankie and Johnny* 3. Leopard 4. Splash! 5. Lauren Bacall 6. Rudolph Valentino 7. *Moonstruck* 8. At a train station 9. Joseph Fiennes 10. Cameron Diaz

QUIZ 282

• •

The answer to each of the following questions begins with the letter B.

1   In which movie did Woody Allen find himself embroiled in a South American rebellion?

2   Which Gene Kelly musical features the song, 'The Heather on the Hill'?

3   In which 2000 comedy did Brendan Fraser sign away his soul to the devil?

4   Which animated deer was introduced to the big screen in 1942 by the Disney studios?

5   In which 1996 movie did David Bowie portray Andy Warhol?

6   Which 1995 movie told the story of anorphaned piglet adopted by a sheepdog?

7   Which 1997 comedy was directed by Mel Smith and co-starred John Mills?

8   In which 1988 picture did Robert Loggia play Tom Hanks' boss?

9   What is the title of the 1992 movie that starred a St. Bernard dog?

10   Which 1989 movie was set in Gotham City?

ANSWERS

1. Bananas   2. Brigadoon   3. Bedazzled   4. Bambi   5. Basquiat   6. Babe
7. Bean   8. Big   9. Beethoven   10. Batman

QUIZ 283

• •

1 In which 2002 movie does Paul Newman play a Mafia boss called John Rooney?

2 Who was nominated for a Best Actor Oscar for his role in the *The Stuntman*?

3 Who played a sleazy investigator in the comedy *There's Something about Mary*?

4 Which actor played the lead role in the 1990 flop *Almost an Angel*?

5 Which Canadian-born star married Douglas Fairbanks Sr.?

6 What type of bird is Fawkes in the *Harry Potter* movies?

7 Which 1977 Disney movie featured a dragon called Elliot?

8 In which movie did Karen Dotrice play Jane Banks?

9 On whose novel was *Jaws* based?

10 Who played Clouseau in *The Pink Panther*?

ANSWERS

1. *The Road to Perdition* 2. Peter O'Toole 3. Matt Dillon 4. Paul Hogan
5. Mary Pickford 6. Phoenix 7. Pete's Dragon 8. *Mary Poppins* 9. Peter
Benchley 10. Peter Sellers

QUIZ 284

• •

1 Who played Lex Luthor in three *Superman* movies?

2 In what year was Christopher Reeve paralyzed in a horse-riding accident?

3 By what name was Superman known as a baby?

4 For what newspaper does Clark Kent work?

5 Which actor plays Otis, Lex Luthor's hapless sidekick?

6 Who received a reported $3 million fee for a ten-minute appearance as Superman's father?

7 Which British actress played Superman's mother in *Superman II*?

8 Which character is played by Margot Kidder in the *Superman* movies?

9 What was the subtitle of *Superman IV*?

10 Who composed the music for the 1978 movie?

ANSWERS

1. Gene Hackman 2. 1995 3. Kal-El 4. *The Daily Planet* 5. Ned Beatty
6. Marlon Brando 7. Susannah York 8. Lois Lane 9. *The Quest for Peace*
.10. John Williams

QUIZ 285

- -

1 Who played Batman in the 1989 movie *Batman* and in *Batman Returns* in 1992?

2 Which star of the 2000 movie *Charlie's Angels* played Sugar in *Batman Forever*?

3 Who played Batgirl in *Batman and Robin*?

4 How is the character of Oswald Cobblepot better known?

5 What is the name of the villain played by Tommy Lee Jones in *Batman Forever*?

6 Who played Batman in the 1966 picture and the 1960s TV series?

7 Which foe of Batman was portrayed on screen by Arnold Schwarzenegger?

8 Which character was played on TV by Burt Ward and on screen by Chris O'Donnell?

9 Who played newspaper reporter Vicki Vale in the 1989 *Batman* movie?

10 Who directed the 1989 movie and its 1992 sequel?

ANSWERS

1. Michael Keaton 2. Drew Barrymore 3. Alicia Silverstone 4. The Penguin
5. Two-Face 6. Adam West 7. Mr. Freeze 8. Robin 9. Kim Basinger 10. Tim Burton

QUIZ 286

• •

1 What is the title of the 1999 sequel to *Gregory's Girl*?

2 Which actor connects *The Wild Geese*, *Gold* and *Shout at the Devil*?

3 Which star received the Irving Thalberg Award at the 2000 Oscar ceremonies?

4 Hugh Hudson directed which Oscar-winning picture of the 1980s?

5 Who did Dennis Quaid portray in *Great Balls of Fire*?

6 Which 1992 movie featured the characters of Uncas, Chingachgook and Hawkeye?

7 Which musical features a man-eating plant called Audrey II?

8 Who played the role of M in the 1983 Bond movie, *Never Say Never Again*?

9 Which musical features 'The Time Warp'?

10 Which star of the TV series *Starsky and Hutch* directed *The Running Man*?

ANSWERS

1. *Gregory's Two Girls* 2. Roger Moore 3. Warren Beatty 4. *Chariots of Fire*
5. Jerry Lee Lewis 6. *The Last of the Mohicans* 7. *Little Shop of Horrors*
8. Edward Fox 9. *The Rocky Horror Picture Show* 10. Paul Michael Glaser

QUIZ 287

. . . .

1 Which actress connects Copycat, Dave and *Working Girl*?

2 Which British Dame won an Oscar for her role in *A Passage to India*?

3 Which novel by Tom Wolfe was turned into a movie starring Tom Hanks and Bruce Willis?

4 Which 1990 picture featured a pair of hapless burglars called Harry and Marv?

5 Who sang the theme for the 1984 movie, *Footloose*?

6 In *The Lion King* who wrote the lyrics for the Oscar-winning song, 'Circle of Life'?

7 Meryl Streep played Karen Blixen in which 1985 Oscar-winning picture?

8 Which 1962 musical sees Cliff Richard driving a double-decker bus?

9 Which 1978 movie starring Barbra Streisand had been made in 1937 and again in 1954?

10 Which 1978 musical is set at Rydell High School?

ANSWERS

QUIZ 288

• •

1   In which movie did Robin Williams find himself imprisoned in a board game?

2   He earned his first Oscar nomination for which picture?

3   What is the title of the 1999 movie in which Williams plays a robot?

4   In what decade was he born?

5   When Williams played Popeye who played Olive Oyl?

6   Which movie, based on a true story, saw him playing an unconventional doctor?

7   Which 1997 picture earned Williams a Best Supporting Actor Oscar?

8   Williams sings 'Friend like me' in which 1992 movie?

9   In which picture does he play a tramp who was once a medieval historian?

10 DEPOSITED TEA COSY is an anagram of which movie starring Williams?

ANSWERS

1. *Jumanji* 2. *Good Morning Vietnam* 3. Bicentennial Man 4. 1950s – born in 1952 5. Shelley Duvall 6. Patch Adams 7. *Good Will Hunting* 8. Aladdin, as the voice of the Genie 9. *The Fisher King* 10. *Dead Poets Society*

QUIZ 289

• •

1 Julia Roberts co-starred with Richard Gere for the second time in which movie?

2 Beginning with F, what is Julia's middle name?

3 In which 1991 fantasy did she play Tinkerbell?

4 In which 1997 movie is Mel Gibson helped by Julia to overcome his paranoia?

5 Which 2000 picture earned Julia her first Best Actress Oscar?

6 Which actor became engaged to Julia in 1990?

7 In the movie Sleeping with the Enemy, who played her abusive husband?

8 What is the first name of the character played by Julia in *Pretty Woman*?

9 MIX THE CANE is an anagram of which movie starring Julia?

10 Which film co-starred Julia Roberts and Cameron Diaz as Julianne Potter and Kimberly Wallace?

ANSWERS

1. *Runaway Bride* 2. Fiona 3. *Hook* 4. Conspiracy Theory 5. *Erin Brockovich*
6. Kiefer Sutherland 7. Patrick Bergin 8. Vivian 9. *The Mexican* 10. *My Best Friends Wedding*

QUIZ 290

. . . .

Unravel the anagrams to reveal the names of ten male
movie stars.

1 PROFANE TED

2 BURRLY MAIL

3 BEWARE TYRANT

4 A LION CAP

5 DUPED MY HEIR

6 OLD WEST ACTION

7 BIG MELONS

8 SEAL COACHING

9 MOIST CURE

10 BLAST CRY LILY

ANSWERS

QUIZ 291

• •

Unravel the anagrams to reveal the names of ten
    female movie stars.

1   HEALING JET

2   DIETS FOR JOE

3   DREAM BRINGING

4   MERRY WARDROBE

5   HONEST ARSON

6   LEN THE HUN

7   SAME WET

8   BATH AT KEYS

9   A NEWEST KILT

10   DO DIARYS

ANSWERS

1. Janet Leigh 2. Jodie Foster 3. Ingrid Bergman 4. Drew Barrymore
5. Sharon Stone 6. Helen Hunt 7. Mae West 8. Kathy Bates 9. Kate Winslet
10. Doris Day

QUIZ 292

. . . .

1 Who played Dracula in the spoof horror, *Dracula: Dead and Loving It*?

2 Joshua, Michael and Heather are the main characters in which 1999 horror flick?

3 Which series of horror flicks feature an evil character known as Pinhead?

4 Which 1983 movie, based on a novel, tells the story of a car possessed with an evil spirit?

5 In which 1985 comedy horror did Michael J. Fox play a werewolf?

6 In which 1999 movie is Johnny Depp terrorized by a headless horseman?

7 What is the title of the 1997 sequel to *An American Werewolf in London*?

8 Who plays the title role in the horror *Dracula 2000*?

9 Which 1979 movie with James Brolin featured the occupants of a haunted house?

10 Who played the possessed child Regan in the horror classic *The Exorcist*?

ANSWERS

1. Leslie Nielsen 2. *The Blair Witch Project* 3. *Hellraiser* 4. *Christine*
5. *Teenwolf* 6. *Sleepy Hollow* 7. *An American Werewolf in Paris* 8. Gerard
Butler 9. *The Amityville Horror* 10. Linda Blair

QUIZ 293

. . . .

1 Which 1987 thriller featured a married couple called Dan and Beth Gallagher?

2 In which movie is Jodie Foster terrorized by three intruders at her New York home?

3 Which 1991 thriller featured an evil nanny called Peyton Flanders?

4 Who played a police detective in the crime thrillers *Seven* and *Kiss the Girls*?

5 Which action thriller features Vinnie Jones and Nicholas Cage as a pair of car thieves?

6 What is the name of the CIA agent played by Harrison Ford in *Patriot Games*?

7 Which 1999 psychological thriller featured Bruce Willis and Samuel L. Jackson?

8 In which 1972 movie did Burt Reynolds and Jon Voight embark on a nightmare canoe trip?

9 Who connects the thrillers *Spy Game*, *Three Days of the Condor* and *Legal Eagles*?

10 In which movie did Will Smith play Robert Dean, a lawyer who is framed for murder?

ANSWERS

1. Fatal Attraction 2. Panic Room 3. The Hand that Rocks the Cradle
4. Morgan Freeman 5. Gone in 60 Seconds 6. Jack Ryan 7. Unbreakable
8. Deliverance 9. Robert Redford 10. Enemy of the State

QUIZ 294

• •

1 What is Michael Caine's real name?

2 He took his stage surname from which comedy starring Humphrey Bogart?

3 In which 1988 comedy did Caine and Steve Martin play a pair of conmen?

4 In which acclaimed drama did Caine play the role of Dr. Wilbur Larch?

5 In which 1998 movie did he co-star with Jane Horrocks?

6 Which 2002 film set in the 1950s, earned Caine a Best Actor Oscar nomination for his role as Thomas Fowler?

7 Which Camden pop group had a hit with a song entitled "Michael Caine"?

8 Name the star who played the title role in a 2000 remake of the 1971 movie Get Carter.

9 Who did Caine play in The Muppets Christmas Carol?

10 What rank was the character played by Caine in the movie Zulu?

ANSWERS

1. Maurice Micklewhite 2. The Caine Mutiny 3. Dirty Rotten Scoundrels
4. The Cider House Rules 5. Little Voice 6. The Quiet American
7. Madness 8. Sylvester Stallone 9. Ebenezer Scrooge 10. Lieutenant

QUIZ 295

1 Who played Frank Sinatra in the 1998 biopic, The Rat Pack?

2 Which 1953 movie earned Sinatra an Oscar for his portrayal of Sergeant Maggio?

3 In which 1956 film did Frank Sinatra sing, "You're Sensational"?

4 Which "rat pack" movie of 1960 was remade in 2001 starring George Clooney?

5 Who was Sinatra married to from 1951 to 1954?

6 In which 1965 war movie did he play a prisoner killed trying to escape on a train?

7 Which capital city provides the surname for the detective played by Sinatra in 1965?

8 In which 1956 musical did he sing the song, 'Adelaide'?

9 What 1963 movie saw Sinatra bound for the second largest state in the U.S.A.?

10 Which Sinatra sang the theme song of the James Bond movie *You Only Live Twice*?

ANSWERS

1. Ray Liotta 2. From Here to Eternity 3. High Society 4. Ocean's Eleven
5. Ava Gardner 6. Von Ryan's Express 7. Rome – Tony Rome 8. Guys and
Dolls 9. Four For Texas 10. Nancy Sinatra – his daughter

QUIZ 296

. . . .

1 In which country is *Doctor Zhivago* set?

2 Who directed the picture?

3 Who played the role of Pasha Antipova in *Dr Zhivago*?

4 On whose novel was *Doctor Zhivago* based?

5 What is the first name of *Doctor Zhivago*?

6 Which British star played Lara in *Doctor Zhivago*?

7 During which war was the movie set?

8 Who played General Zhivago in the movie?

9 In what year of the 1960s was the picture released?

10 What is the first name of the character played by Geraldine Chaplin?

ANSWERS

1. Russia 2. David Lean 3. Tom Courtenay 4. Boris Pasternak 5. Yuri
6. Julie Christie 7. World War I 8. Alec Guinness 9. 1965 10. Tonya

QUIZ 297

• •

1　On which Shakespeare play was *West Side Story* based?

2　Who played the leading lady Maria in the movie?

3　In which year of the 1960s was the movie made?

4　Who jointly directed the musical West Side Story and went on to direct *The Sound Of Music*?

5　Who composed the music for the movie?

6　In which city is West Side Story set?

7　Who won a Best Supporting Actor Oscar for his portrayal of the gang leader Riff?

8　Which song contains the line, "I like the city of San Juan. I know a boat you can get on"?

9　How many Oscars did *West Side Story* win?

10　Whose singing voice does the soprano Marnie Nixon overdub?

ANSWERS

1. Romeo and Juliet 2. Natalie Wood 3. 1961 4. Robert Wise 5. Leonard Bernstein 6. New York 7. George Chakaris 8. "America" 9. Ten 10. Natalie Wood's

QUIZ 298

1 Which 2003 movie sees Nick Nolte playing the father of Dr. Bruce Banner?

2 Which actor was America's most decorated soldier of World War II?

3 Who played the writer Joan Wilder in both *Romancing the Stone* and *Jewel of the Nile*?

4 In which movie did Jennifer Grey play the character of Baby Houseman?

5 Elliot Carver is the name of the villain in which Bond movie?

6 Which 1990 movie features Leonardo, Michelangelo, Donatello and Raphael?

7 In which 1982 comedy did Dustin Hoffman play the characters of Michael and Dorothy?

8 Which singing legend played the owner of a beauty salon in *Steel Magnolias*?

9 In which movie did Elton John sing 'Pinball Wizard'?

10 Who plays the role of Leo Getz in the *Lethal Weapon* movies?

ANSWERS

1. Hulk 2. Audie Murphy 3. Kathleen Turner 4. *Dirty Dancing* 5. *Tomorrow Never Dies* 6. *Teenage Mutant Ninja Turtles* 7. *Tootsie* 8. Dolly Parton 9. *Tommy* 10. Joe Pesci

QUIZ 299

• •

1. Which 1995 movie saw Ted Danson searching for a Scottish monster?

2. Which 2001 comedy saw Whoopi Goldberg, Rowan Atkinson and Cuba Gooding Jnr in a race for $2 million?

3. Which American wrestler plays the title role in the 2002 movie *The Scorpion King*?

4. Which *Carry On* star became the landlady of The Queen Vic in *EastEnders*?

5. In a 1984 movie, who did Linda Lee turn into when donning a red cape?

6. In the Stuart Little movies what kind of animal was Stuart Little?

7. Which 1984 gangster flick was based on a novel called *The Hoods*?

8. Who played the Martian in the 1999 picture *My Favorite Martian*?

9. Which sleuth did Margaret Rutherford portray in the thriller *Murder Most Foul*?

10. Who plays the role of Zed in the *Men in Black* movies?

ANSWERS

1. Loch Ness 2. *Rat Race* 3. *The Rock* – Dwayne Johnson 4. Barbara Windsor
5. Supergirl 6. A white mouse 7. *Once Upon a Time in America*
8. Christopher Lloyd 9. Miss Marple 10. Rip Torn

QUIZ 300

. . . .

1 Which star's first name means "fresh breeze coming down from the mountains"?

2 Bert and Ernie from *Sesame Street* were named after characters from which movie?

3 In *The Thirty-Nine Steps*, who has been played by Robert Powell and Kenneth More?

4 Which 1930s movie was the first picture to have its sequel released in the same year?

5 Which Oscar winner holds the title of "Baron of Richmond upon Thames"?

6 Which star said, "If I'd have known that, I'd have put on an eye patch 35 years ago"?

7 Who connects *The Swiss Family Robinson*, *The Vikings* and *King of Kings*?

8 Who became the first star to win an Oscar for a performance in a foreign language?

9 Which star of *Coronation Street* went on to become an Oscar-winning actor?

10 What was used to simulate blood in Alfred Hitchcock's *Psycho*?

ANSWERS

1. Keanu Reeves 2. *It's a Wonderful Life* 3. Richard Hannay 4. *King Kong*, both made in 1933 5. Richard Attenborough 6. John Wayne 7. All narrated by Orson Welles 8. Sophia Loren 9. Ben Kingsley 10. Chocolate syrup